BLACK POWER

&

white cower, Inc.

written by a U.S. government-
approved white coward

DR. J. ELLWOOD AUGELLO

ISBN 978-1-961227-07-1 (paperback)
ISBN 978-1-961227-08-8 (digital)

Rushmore Press LLC
1 800 460 9188
www.rushmorepress.com

Printed in the United States of America

For my folks, John and Mildred, and my
brother Don—
may you all rest in peace.

In response to
U.S. Attorney General Eric H. Holder, Jr.,
a black man who said this about whites
and race issues in America:
"...and we, I believe, continue to be in too
many ways essentially a nation of cowards."
New York Times, March 8, 2009

and inspired by
Steven Yates, white author of "Civil Wrongs—
What Went Wrong with Affirmative Action"

and further instigated by
Ralph Wiley, black author of "Why
Black People Tend to Shout"

TABLE OF CONTENTS

PACOIMA

"Eny, meeny, miney, moe, catch a nigger by his toe..." suddenly, my voice trailed off and I noticed an eerie silence, interrupted by a few muffled chuckles. I then looked up and saw my Little League Baseball Coach Merkenson's face, which had a combined look of concern and bewilderment.

He finally interrupted my "racial" singsong and spoke to me, saying it would be better if I would use another method to pick sides for our practice game.

It was 1958, and I was twelve years old and playing for the Dodgers in the San Fernando Little League, a youth baseball organization located in a small town that was situated just north of Los Angeles, California. I was co-captain of the team, along with my good friend, Craig Merkenson, the coach's son.

Earlier in the practice that day, I had been asked by our coach, a well-liked man in his late thirties, to randomly pick players for two practice teams. Without thinking, I mimicked a selection method I had previously heard from older white guys in my neighborhood in Pacoima, which was a small town next to San Fernando.

Subsequently, after saying the word "nigger," I sort of realized it was a poor choice of words when picking sides for our practice teams, especially after seeing the look on Mr. Merkenson's face. Our coach, without hesitation, hastily moved the practice session forward after I whispered a sincere short apology to him.

He then took me aside, grabbed my shoulder, and said: "Remember, you're a leader of this team," which had a rambunctious

1

mixture of white kids, a Mexican, and a few blacks. I sighed and moved on with practice. It was so many years ago, but I remember it like it was yesterday.

Frankly, to this day, I still thank Mr. Merkenson for not causing that awkward moment to become a bigger scene. Even my friend Craig, his son, came up to me and reminded me not to say "nigger" too loud in certain parts of Pacoima, which had three distinct tough neighborhoods of poor blacks, poor Mexicans, and poor "white trash." Craig's advice seemed appropriate, since he, like his father, was black.

Such was the mixed-race life in Pacoima and its surrounding areas in the 1950s. We were diverse and had ambivalent neighbors, who all knew their boundaries. But we did interact together in sports and other activities. For example, one such interactive activity was when we whites would always run like hell through a dangerous part of a black or Mexican neighborhood after dark.

Overall, we all wanted to co-exist in a rough and tumble life of "friendly" survival in a lower economic and social world. Personally, I thought we were all just a bunch of good-natured and struggling occupants of old Pacoima, and all of us, including my parents, were dreaming about when we would get the hell out of Pacoima.

A DIGRESSION

Before I get into my own story about modern-day American racial escapades, involving Black Power and white cower, I've inserted the following essay that my older brother, Don, who was battling social and racial demons, wrote in 1969. After reading it, I hope you'll understand why I am frankly angered at some of the asinine and self-serving affirmative actions of "we shall overcome all you white mother-fuckers and kill your privileged white shit!" I'm also ashamed I didn't help my older brother when he needed it, especially after all the years he guided and supported me.

My beloved brother, who "accidentally overdosed" at too young an age in 2000, had left some of his possessions and writings with me. Years after he died, I started looking through his stuff and discovered a long essay that he had written and submitted to Look Magazine for publication.

As added background to his essay, I want you to know that my brother was a humble and very talented gentle giant, who excelled at everything that he attempted, and he displayed a gracious demeanor to all people—no matter what their color or beliefs.

Although after reading my brother's essay, I was both surprised and very upset that he harbored such deep and troubling emotions over the issues of race. I have included his essay in this short manuscript to show how an overly zealous and politically correct part of society screwed up my very decent brother.

There are parts of this essay that make me want to puke because I knew my brother pretty well and I personally feel that the writing of his deep personal racial conflicts was the gut-wrenching product of a guilt-ridden and ethnic thumping on his vulnerable state of mind. He, along with other vulnerable naïve white WWII war babies, had received the cultural passing-on-down undeserving wrath of the manufactured sins of their so-called privileged white American fathers, like our combat veteran father, who later lived in an era of post-World War II trauma and the combined guilt of surviving a devastating war and then later being confronted with the U.S. government's social programs of blaming all whites for anachronistic 200 year-old black slavery issues.

After fighting, killing, and having friends and comrades killed by other persons who possessed different cultures, beliefs, and "colors," these American fathers struggled to gain future peace and prosperity as they quietly possessed a tolerant state of mind, which insulated them from other people of different colors and cultures in their own country. An obvious exception being in America's Deep South where white people and other people of a different color had some real serious problems between them.

For me, I was always known to have a rebellious loose screw or two, so the racial and cultural guilt trips mostly passed by me in my younger days because of a personal Southern California philosophy of "We're all mixed together according to some crazy cosmic plan. and we are all slaves to someone or something, so who gives a shit as long as we can all survive peacefully and regularly body surf at Zuma Beach."

As previously mentioned, the following essay was my brother's submission to Look magazine in 1969.

"A Short Autobiography of a White Racist" by Don Angello

1943-52

Nigger baby! Ya dirty nigger baby! Ha, ha, ha. "Eenie, meenie, mynie, moe. Catch a nigger by the toe..." By the way, a "nigger toe" was my favorite nut. Brazilian nut? What was that, a crazy South American? Probably somebody with a nigger nose, nigger lips, and curly steel wool for nigger hair.

"Get that dirty penny out of your mouth," yelled mom, "You never know if a nigger touched it. Why don't you act like the white American you are!"

> Did I as a child ever see Blacks? Yes, but my poor white neighborhood was taboo for "such as them." Thus, an early education of sayings, clichés, jokes, and name-calling formed my ignorant views and warped my attitudes toward all non-whites, especially Blacks.

1952-61

Go back to Africa, jungle bunnies! Look at those funny-looking creeps. "…and God forgot to make them white."

Willy Mays just can't break Babe Ruth's record! If anyone does, I hope to hell Mickey Mantle or some other white baseball player does it.

Basketball has also gone to the jigaboos. Just look at the starting five on any team. It's a crying shame. And football is a problem, too. Too bad for the sport. Why, some football teams have seven or more in both the defensive and offensive starting line-ups! And boxing? Forget it. After Rocky Marciano quit, the sport suffered from the Black plague. My God, something ought to be done. They're taking over everything!

Even though many of them are great athletes, none of them have any brains. How many Black quarterbacks are around?

Only have one nigger at my Catholic high school. Must admit, he is a riot. But any coon is funny as hell, as long as he knows his place. All of them are like foreigners or Martians. Could be a lower-level animal group, you know, like first cousins to baboons. Anyway, niggers are outside the real world, that's for sure.

Glad as hell I'm not on the outside looking in like them. No matter how bad things ever got to be, I could always be thankful I was white!

"How much in white man's money?" is one of my favorite sayings. If anyone's clothes are ripped, torn, or in bright loud colors, I can cut him down with "Was it hard to catch him?" or "Where'd you find him?" both sayings meaning a living or dead nigger. Giving the correct time of day as "white man's time" always gets a chuckle. And Rastus and Liza jokes are like "Amos and Andy" nigger stories.

Seriously now, the only good nigger is a dead nigger! But they are good for some fucking fine jokes. You call a Negro with a Ph.D. and a million dollars a "nigger," but you call a seven-foot nigger with a weapon "Sir!"

I guess they really are okay, just as long as they don't get uppity. Hell, I've got a few Negro friends, and I'm not prejudiced against them, as long as I don't see them with a white woman.

After all, there are some damned good ones around. Too bad they have to suffer because of the rest of the lazy bastards. Really, too bad the good ones aren't white. At least the good ones sure try to be. Christ, I wouldn't be a nigger for anything.

Black bastards! Wish to Christ we could send them back where they belong. I'd shoot any one of them if he came near my sister or daughter. The same goes for their nigger-loving commie friends, those fucking "Freedom Riders." They're crazy and should get their asses killed. Why, I know niggers just want to be with their own— same as us, dammit!

By the way, it's about time someone put a bullet in that Malcolm X. Imagine a nigger talking like that? Surprised he lasted so long. Maybe now that commie Martin Luther King will wise up.

Must be communism behind all this nigger crap. Thank God for the KKK!

Los Angeles, California at its best! That was my warped thinking from childhood through high school. How could anyone overcome eighteen solid years of that crap?! My only real contact with Blacks was in the expanding world of school sports. Fortunately, it opened up a racially diversified environment for me. My going to UCLA was a dramatic change in many ways, yet only slowly did my liberation begin.

1961-64

I just cannot believe those white college girls dating or being seen with a colored guy. Don't they realize what it does to their reputations? The only reason a colored boy wants to be with a white girl is for her to be a feather in his coonskin cap. And I know the only reason a white girl goes out with a coon is that she wants his big prick. What if her family found out? Would tear them up. White nigger whores!

College sure messes up some people's minds. Wait until those nigger-lovers get into the real world. They are nothing but white troublemakers who don't know how to mind their own business, like some people's business could be dangerous business, especially when it comes to desegregation and all that other integration shit. They must be pretty dumb or something if they can't see that people are people and will always be the same.

Sure, I'm for civil rights, but the Negroes are pushing too hard. You just don't change things overnight. You can't have everything all at once. Besides, look what the Irish and Italians did for themselves in such a short time, even after suffering discrimination problems when they first arrived in America. Why can't Negroes make it the way my people did, through education and hard work? They'd better wise up, or else somebody's gonna have to wise them up. After all, whites out-number the blacks in America ten to one.

I had dropped out of UCLA after two years to play professional baseball with the Los Angeles Dodgers. It was at this point I read my first book on my own, at the age of twenty-one. My mind had finally begun to open up a little by the time I arrived in Florida for spring training at Vero Beach in 1965.

1965

They what?! They wouldn't let a fellow player named Ted use the town's Laundromat to wash his clothes. In Florida? Man, I don't believe it! So this is what prejudice is all about. Hell, I'd almost let a good Negro like Ted date my sister. Son of a bitch, what a bummer, Ted.

Wow, what a crowd at today's ball game! One side of the bleachers looked like it was an African Convention, with only black folks there sitting and watching the game. Now I can see what segregation is all about from first-hand experience. What a shock. Now I can understand what both responsible and radical civil rights leaders are talking about. At least we don't have this sort of thing in the North and West of America. Isn't that right, Ted?

Yet most of the agitation crap is definitely communist-inspired. Why, there's documented proof that Martin Luther King was a communist. I just wish they'd all be like the good sensible Negroes on our sports teams. Of course, even they get pretty damned uppity sometimes. Christ, why couldn't things have been left alone? Everything was just fine for everyone until…

Now they've really done it! Don't the 1965 Watts riots in Los Angeles show what those colored people will do with their so-called civil rights? They even shot Dick Gregory, one of their own kind. Too bad they don't see what could happen in an all-out racial battle since the odds are ten to one in our white favor.

Besides, it's only a small minority that's usually causing all the trouble. My friend's cleaning lady says that most of her people don't want any trouble and that everything was just fine before. Man, they're really getting out of hand. Something drastic ought to be done, and fast. As for me, my rifle and pistol are ready for action, if that's what they want.

> Baseball didn't work out and I returned to UCLA to finish a Bachelor's degree. By this time, I was reading at what was for me an incredible pace. My first real step in understanding my racism occurred during the summer after my first semester back at UCLA.

1966-67

An unbearable fifty-hour summer bus ride to Iowa to visit relatives had two unforeseen results.

A fellow traveler, a college freshman of seventeen, had used a considerable amount of knowledge of philosophy, with a particular emphasis on Nietzche, to finally help me break through the intellectual fetters of my discarded hang-ups of Catholicism and a four-year mental hangover from my previous dark years of white conservative bullshit.

On the same trip, I read my first book on the Negro movement in the U.S., called "Black Nationalism" by E.U. Essien-Udom. I could not believe how ignorant I had been concerning the American Negro, especially in light of the developments since 1950. I was amazed at what there was to know about the Black people in my country, about their movements, and about Black leaders, such as Marcus Garvey, Elijah Muhammad, and Malcolm X.

Stupid opinions and warped viewpoints were rapidly broken down, and discarded and reformed during my following year at UCLA. One of my courses required two important books for a broad background of knowledge about the Negro problems in the United States. Arnold Rose's condensation of Gunnar Myrdal's "The American Dilemma" revealed the magnitude and ugliness of our racial problems. I grew into a partial understanding of white oppression and black "powerlessness." Negro rioting no longer seemed a mystery. Stokely Carmichael and H. Rap Brown were beginning to make more sense to me.

The other required book for the course at UCLA was Stanley M. Elkins' "Slavery." No romanticized Hollywood presentation of plantation life and slavery here. My questions as to why the Negro's difficulties with American society differed from the Irish or Italian experiences were being answered. The Negro's culture, family, and individuality were destroyed by slavery. I began to understand why American Black people had so much to overcome in order to make it in our society. But not only by rioting, that's for certain!

Then I heard Louis Lomax speak at UCLA on the riots. From that point on, I was convinced that he was correct in stating that a real racial revolution was going on in America. His reasoning and views as detailed in his book, "The Negro Revolt," opened a new dimension of the black movement. Even the riots now made sense, and I felt an understanding of sorts with radical blacks such as Bobby Seale, whom I also heard at UCLA.

Yet, I was still a racist. Having never thought of myself as being either racist or prejudiced, I could not see the problem within myself. The black man's enemy was "out there," like in the American South. Even with new knowledge and understanding, I still found it easy to feel distant from any black person and feel strange in his presence. My enlightenment stopped short of accepting a Negro as an equal human being in every respect. My racist society did an excellent job on me, with long-lasting results. I was almost a finished and forever ignorant product.

Fortunately, the summer of my graduation from UCLA saw a great change in my head. I fell in with some hip people and was initiated into a conscious attempt at changing myself. Along with those important people, books such as "It's Happening," "The Adjusted American," "The Wisdom of Insecurity," "Psychological Studies in Zen Thought," "The True Believer," "The Naked Ape,"

"On Aggression," and others, broke down narrow vistas and opened new horizons.

However, the following graduate year of study at UCLA was one of inner struggles with near-fatal consequences. Depression and suicidal tendencies left little room for conscious efforts at furthering my self-improvement. Self-preservation was the order of the day.

> A three-month trip to Europe set me on a revised path of recovery and, quite incidentally, resulted in a new breakthrough with my racist problems.

1968

Two months of getting outside my American shell in Europe was a much-needed retreat and also a necessary preparation for an important event that happened while I was in Copenhagen.

Copenhagen had previously set a beautiful tone by working within and throughout my mind and soul. I was feeling the most complete "people trip" I had ever experienced. Brotherhood of man and enlightenment seemed to take on real meaning.

I was in the Tivoli Gardens on a people-watching stroll, where fellow strollers seemed to personify and verify my inner feelings when it happened.

What a sudden jolt to my previous closed-mindedness. I noticed a good-looking, happy couple walking leisurely along with their baby in a stroller. Pow! It took a few moments for it to sink in that he was black, she was white, and the baby was somewhere in-between. My eventual reaction to their color difference was one of pleasant surprise, after my mind surpassed the initial feelings of disbelief over their very black-and-white differences.

It was this pleasant non-reaction to their racial differences that stopped me in my tracks. My normal reaction would have been a double-take and saying to myself: "Why the fuck is that white girl with a black?" Yet this time, I only perceived a young couple and their child, and I did not take a what-the-fuck double take because of their different racial backgrounds.

A wonderful sensation of triumph rushed to my head and a warm glow welled up through my body. What a beautiful atmosphere the people of Copenhagen have created! And I was lucky enough to experience it in person.

Unfortunately, there was an ever-nagging catch. My personal breakthrough was inspired from without and, later, I could not continue to feel within the atmosphere I had felt in Copenhagen. In my gut, I remained apart from the intellectual appreciation of my triumphant personal experience in the Tivoli Gardens.

Even so, a few more books and some more direct experiences in Europe came to further my rescue from ignorance and racism. Toward the end of my trip, the reading of "The Autobiography of Malcolm X" threw me into my first intimate experience with a black person. Malcolm X was the first to begin liberating my gut from so many external, poisonous, and humanly mutilating feelings and attitudes toward blacks. That great man still lives and I hope for a long time.

From that point on, instead of reading about black people from the pen of white scholars, and listening to the white man's interpretations, explanations, and answers to the plight of black people, I decided to seek the light from the source, like Malcolm X. To experience Black people and their revolution, I came to realize that meaningful help could come only from Black people.

> Immediately after my return from Europe to Los Angeles, I moved to San Francisco, a city I thought comparable to Copenhagen in many respects. Soon, I married an American-Jewish lady and returned to graduate school to finish a secondary teaching credential and start on a Master's degree.

1968-69

In my conversations with Europeans about "Third World" peoples, particularly Blacks in the U.S., the name Frantz Fanon was mentioned and his writings were recommended. After settling in San Francisco, I read "The Wretched of the Earth." By gaining insight into the psychology of oppressed peoples and their oppressors, I began to comprehend the real psychology of racism.

"Soul on Ice" and "Black Rage" exposed that evil more clearly and further helped to open my insides for my own reflective evaluations. I realized that racism, the great enemy of brotherhood, was built into the psychological make-up and culture of white Americans. How could I possibly exorcise the demon racism from within my existence and outside my personal sphere?

My salvation from such a deep cultural curse continued through my open friendships with some understanding blacks. First, there was a black married couple with whom my wife and I exchanged dinner dates at home. My wife and I found it strange that black people had basically the same hopes, worries, cares, fears, etc., as we did. Much to my surprise, I also found that we could talk to them as individual persons, not as a Black couple.

My greatest progress came with the friendship of my wife's close white friend's Black mate. He was sensitive to my struggle and handled our get-togethers in a beautiful way. I could eventually see the man as a man, not as a Black man. More importantly, I grew to view the couple not as black and white, but as two persons in love. Happily, my wife and I had been able to expand on these and other experiences in order to view people and situations in a color-blind light.

Whereas my liberation from racism had been a slow process for obvious reasons, my wife's more rapid progress had been due to primarily her liberal Jewish upbringing by her then-single mother. As a child, she was never allowed to use the word "nigger" and was spared the meaner trappings of American racism. Her mother's later divorce from a WASP husband had started my wife to compare viewpoints between conservative and liberal mindsets.

I do find it interesting to note the differences between my wife and her later WASP half-brother and half-sisters regarding typical American racist views and word usage. My wife's stepfather had raised his children with most of the racist trappings my wife missed at her earlier single mother's home.

My wife's basically Jewish upbringing and influence had been a necessary ally in my victory over racism. But that victory is not without its negative legacy.

Initially, there was so much more to understand. Previous readings, college courses, and travels had opened my mind, as well as direct personal experiences with blacks. Even so, the surface had been just slightly dented. Time and continued efforts will root out the racist evil within me and fill the void with understanding.

The second and most disturbing legacy was more subtle and much more difficult to deal with. Now I experience an overreaction on my part when I come into direct contact with blacks. What deep guilt complexes were at work here? Will I be plagued until the end of my days by a dehumanizing past?

The very least I can do is to spare my children the curse of racism, thus sparing humanity added evil and enemies. Hopefully, racism in one's individual family will not survive in the next generation.

San Francisco, Summer, 1969

Thinking of my brother's passionate essay, I try to imagine the debate that transpired when the Look magazine's editorial board discussed the pros and cons of publishing such a controversial piece of writing, especially after the recently enacted U.S. law entitled 'The Civil Rights Act of 1964." The nervous debate most likely focused on the repeated use of the infamous N-word. Look magazine was mostly known for its famous photographs, and I think such a graphic essay on racism was a touchy subject then for its editorial board.

The following are the replies from LOOK in 1970.

LOOK

A PUBLICATION OF COWLES COMMUNICATIONS, INC. 625
MARKET STREET SAN FRANCISCO, CALIF. 94105

May 18, 1970

Mr. Don Angello
801 Corbett Ave., #12
San Francisco, Calif. 94131

Dear Mr. Angello:

Please forgive my long delay in responding to your letter and your Short Autobiography. I agree with Dr. Davis that it has the ring of honesty, and have sent it to our editors in New York to get their opinion. There is a slight chance—not great, but still one worth trying—that they might want to publish it in a shortened, 1,500-word version as a one-page essay.

I'll let you know their reaction as soon as I get it.

Best wishes,
/s/
John Poppy
Senior Editor

JP:lnh

LOOK

A PUBLICATION OF COWLES COMMUNICATIONS, INC. 625
MARKET STREET SAN FRANCISCO, CALIF. 94105

June 5, 1970

Mr. Don Angello
801 Corbett Ave., #12
San Francisco, Calif. 94131

Dear Mr. Angello:

I'm sorry to say that our Editorial
Board has reluctantly decided against
publishing your "Short Autobiography
of a Racist."

They felt it was well done and deals
with an important subject, but they
are accepting very little freelance
material at present, so have asked me
to return the article to you.

Sincerely,
/s/
John Poppy
Senior Editor

JP:lnh
Enclosure

After reading my brother's emotional essay, I can honestly say that our mother would have never said, "Get that dirty penny out of your mouth, you never know if a nigger touched it!"

She was raised on a poor Norwegian farm in Iowa, and after her mother passed away when she was nine, her overwrought father asked her to raise her four younger siblings while he struggled with all the farm chores.

Due to the economic burden facing her father, my mother later left home at seventeen to travel alone to Los Angeles to work as an actor's maid in Hollywood. This development occurred after her "traumatized" friend returned to Iowa and offered her the job. Apparently, the job entailed being chased around the actor's house by the lecherous comedy actor and his equally lecherous cohorts. But my mother was forced to leave home by a struggling father, and she took her seven-dollar award for being her high school's salutatorian and left for Hollywood where dreams and sometimes nightmares came true.

My kind but resilient mom lasted for a year as a fast-footed maid and left to work in a tomato cannery in San Fernando. She eventually married an Italian laborer, who was convinced by his Sicilian mother to leave New York and take his three younger brothers to Southern California in order to avoid joining the Mafia. My very opposite parents, who came from very different ethnic backgrounds, settled in Pacoima in 1939 and were amply surrounded by the previously mentioned mixture of other diverse ethnicities.

Over the years, both my parents worked hard to provide for their three sons and we all embraced our mixed-colored neighbors in Pacoima with mutual respect, which became necessary when everyone was equally struggling in a low-income class melting pot. I remember my mother was always kind and compassionate to everyone she met in her lifetime.

For my brother to accuse her of saying such an unkind thing about Black people tells me how far his tormented mind was warped by white guilt.

Moreover, after reading my brother's emotional essay years later, I also realized why my mentally stressed-out brother pointed a gun at me in 1972 and threatened to shoot me because of what I represented in my "privileged white world." The incident scared the hell out of me and simultaneously made me very sad that his brotherly love for me had turned into a surreal hatred over a socially manufactured era of Black Power over white cower.

I remembered saying to my brother in a resigned voice during that traumatic gun incident, "If you need to do it, then do it to stop your suffering." He stared at me with tears welling up in his eyes and then he suddenly gave me the gun that made me recoil in a moment of panic. Next, my brother mumbled a soul-wrenching plea to shoot him to take him out of his misery. After a short pause, I tried to hug him but he abruptly walked away and I didn't see him again for many years.

Later on, I finally did meet with my brother and we exchanged a mutual love for one another just before he left for Sweden in 1975 to salvage his wrecked soul. He had a messy divorce in San Francisco before he had come back to Los Angles in 1971, and he later remarried a very supportive and caring Swedish lady.

During a stable and blissful time in Sweden, he seemed contented and at peace when we exchanged greeting cards and occasionally spoke on the phone.

But in 2000, I was shocked to hear of his untimely death at too young of age from a broken heart and an accidental overdose of prescribed medicine. This all happened soon after the sudden passing of his devoted wife Anita, and it left me heartbroken.

After all these years since the passing of my brother and, more recently, the deaths of my two parents, I'm trying to salvage my grieving heart. I'm also battling to remove the bitterness toward a modern society that currently thrives on the concept of Minorities, Inc., which indirectly destroyed my brother and other vulnerable whites by continuously shoving unjustifiable racial payback (mostly for profit) and other self-serving hypocritical race theories down innocent white people's throats.

Granted, all races have their good and bad. But the comparison of needless bad actions seems to be lopsided toward a Black Power-grabbing scenario against cowering whites, who could someday explode in mindless retaliation, and then we're back to square one again.

"Eeny, meeny, miney, moe, catch a…As I get older, my bitterness about my brother's mid-life turmoil and his early demise makes it so I still can't let go of my suppressed—although mostly subdued—socio-economic racial anger that nags my inner soul.

As a troubled white coward, I fled the United States in 1978 and began living on a small U.S. commonwealth island in the Western Pacific Ocean, where I currently teach a variety of young and different ethnic students in my advancing age.

I'm married to a Filipina and have two children of mixed color (my first child is half-Pacific Islander Palauan from an earlier marriage). This familial dynamic was not produced by racial guilt but by just simple mutual attraction and wanting to have the joy of raising some nice children in a remote area, far away from major civilizations harvesting racial turmoil.

However, the small island where I live does include a natural racial bias exhibited by the xenophobic indigenous islanders, who feel threatened by the ongoing arrivals of "fleeing white outsiders" from the U.S. mainland and other outsiders from Japan, Philippines, Korea, etc., who are considered an ever-growing minority population.

Regrettably, my children of mixed API-Caucasian ethnicity grew up in a continuous and misguided social struggle for competitive racial supremacy even in "paradise." This can happen between people of one ethnic/cultural persuasion, who display their ambivalent acceptance of other mixed ethnic/cultural children of diverse backgrounds in a present-day world of global interaction and resulting in intimate relationships and marriages between different races.

My own global journey from Pacoima has been filled with both great adventures and gritty misadventures, which have been driven by a need to escape the tumultuous vagaries of a self-serving racial era of every race saying, "We shall overcome!"

Overcome what? To overcome a natural tendency of one group of people to avoid another group of people who possess a different set of obsessive and suppressive cultural lifestyles? Too much of any culture can turn into a toxic cultural disillusionment.

Of course, there are those who can move freely between different ethnicities, but the majority of people in one ethnic group do not possess the open-minded skills of blending in and giving up part of their own cultural identity, which traps "tribal people" in a destructive rut. It has sadly created a confined and blind ethnic rut that makes them feel they have to lash out against other different people and try to overpower them for misguided supremacy.

Maybe this motivation to "overcome" another group of different people is driven by jealousy, laziness, and greed. For instance, there is a current trend to destroy white people as a whole for the past actions of certain white bigots and to eliminate whites because they all somehow possess certain white privileges that people of color don't have.

In relation to America's racial rut, there seems to be a serious attempt to punish all white people for the sins of a certain minority of white people, who worked in a mutually beneficial devil's pact with a certain minority group of colored people to create a cruel slavery era some 200 years ago in America and elsewhere.

Slavery was a business proposition, albeit a nasty one, and it was accomplished by both opportunistic whites and powerful people of color, who wanted profits off the backs of a vulnerable group of their own-colored brothers and sisters.

As it turned out, white people in America fought and killed other white people in the American Civil War in order to free the black slaves around a hundred and sixty years ago. Unfortunately, there was a lingering aftermath of dangerous bias in the Deep South of America, which still exists today.

Amazingly in the late 1800s and the early 1900s, the rest of America began opening its doors to people of all colors, including "unwanted whites" like the Irish, Italians, and others during the rapid expansion of immigration to America.

So, why piss on all the white people and always complain about white privilege when it actually seems to manifest itself into ongoing black privilege? We need to move on and not repeat historical screw-ups and not go crazy with mindless retaliation that just keeps the cyclic racial chaos alive and unwell.

A RANDOM AUTOBIOGRAPHY
OF A WHITE COWARD

1959-1970

After living in Pacoima during my early years, my parents decided in the summer of 1959 to move to San Fernando, California, which was populated by mostly white people and some longtime Mexican residents.

San Fernando was said to be less dangerous than Pacoima because of a severe lack of black folks, who were starting to get restless in Pacoima that later ignited widespread black violence during the Watts riots in 1965.

Although my parents embraced people of all colors and beliefs, they figured it would be a safer environment in San Fernando due to the much whiter ethnic demographics at the time. Overall, it turned out that the white population did possess a simmering racial bias and a protective attitude, which was motivated by an underlying sense of fear of "darkies," who were also simmering to a boiling desire to kick the hell out of some whites over past slavery issues and other nagging Negro issues.

Our family settled in a new housing development in San Fernando on Hubbard Street near Granada Hills, California, which a few months later became famous when Soviet Russian President Nikita Khrushchev took an impromptu tour of a typical and modern Southern California housing development in Granada Hills and our neighborhood. This tour was a last-minute change of President

Khrushchev's itinerary when he was denied his main California wish to visit Disneyland. It was reported Nikita was pissed.

The Russian president's neighborhood visit happened on September 19, 1959, and it quickly spread around our neighborhood due to an advancing movement of official-looking cars and media on our usually quiet street. I rushed down from my house to the intersection of Hubbard and Rincon and pushed through a growing crowd of onlookers with my neighbor friend named Billy. I asked Billy to help me climb up to the top of the street sign for a better view of the approaching motorcade. I straddled the crisscrossed street signs and watch an oncoming long black limousine with a small USSR flag waving on the front fender. The crowd seemed subdued to wave and greet the Soviet leader since at the time, he was an apparent nemesis of America.

The black limo slowed way down to turn the corner right near where I was perched, and I could see Khrushchev's big balding head and unsmiling face in the clear back window as he curiously looked out of the window. I was waving and shouted, "Hey, Nicky!" The front passenger window was halfway down and the Russian passenger seat occupant looked up and turned and said something to Khrushchev behind him in the back seat. The back window rolled down and the big balding round face looked up towards me and he gave me a short wave and smirk.

Wow! President Khrushchev gave me a wave and a half-ass smile!

When I climbed down and watched the motorcade disappear down the road, my friend said he witnessed the quick exchange and it had several people taken aback, since most American crowds at Khrushchev's motorcades had given him frosty exchanges and greetings during his visit to America. I guess I was just a curious kid wanting to get the attention of the iconic Russian President Nicky K!

Although when I later told my dad about the Russian exchange, he joked that I should look out for the CIA who might start tailing me.

From the late 1950s to when I graduated from eighth grade in June of 1960, I attended St. Ferdinand's Catholic Elementary School in San Fernando and was taught by mostly strict nuns.

Right after I graduated from eighth grade, I joined five other young lads who were all recruited at a very young and naïve age to join the priesthood. My parents were surprised because I had shown a keen interest in sports and a starting interest in young ladies.

The recruitment and preparation to leave for the priesthood vocation happened too fast and I soon found myself at the train station in San Fernando early on a late summer morning, waiting for the trip to a priest's seminary in Missouri. My dad kept quiet as we sat on a bench on the departing platform. I finally began to carefully read the seminary's pictorial pamphlets and noticed the severe lack of photos of team sports activities and no sightings of pretty young female coeds.

I then nudged my dad and naively asked about the pamphlets, "Where are the photos of the school's sports programs and girls?"

My dad tried his best to contain his amusement at my lack of knowledge of the priesthood, but he eventually started laughing over the apparent lack of the recruiting priests' full disclosure about the cloistered life of a seminarian and the absence of the birds and the bees, etc. He carefully explained to me, without exposing my obvious ignorance of what the true life of a priest was, that young seminarians spent all their time studying and preparing for a life of the priesthood and its rules of celibacy concerning the opposite sex. I sat quietly for a moment, looked at my dad, and sheepishly inquired, "You mean I can't date any girls there?" My dad shook his head in a negative manner while biting his lip. I then asked in an imploring tone, "Can we go home?"

We arrived home and my surprised mom asked my dad what happened, and my dad waited until I was almost out of earshot, and then replied, "Your son found out he couldn't date at the seminary."

I remembered hearing some muffled laughter and I went back to bed, even laughing at myself for the coming-of-age comedic scene that I had created for my bewildered and amused parents.

Later that same summer before high school, I switched from an impulsive spiritual seminary adventure to a spontaneous worldly adventure. So, I asked two friends of mine, who graduated with me from St. Ferdinand's, to join me on an adventurous bicycle ride from San Fernando to San Diego. It was a 150-mile road trip and would entail several unique obstacles while riding on old bikes.

We lied to our parents and said we would be driven to San Diego and ride our bikes around town with a fellow ex-seminarian of mine, who had lasted only two weeks in Missouri and came back home to San Diego where his parents had moved.

That long round trip on a dilapidated bike made me think again about making radically impulsive decisions, like joining a freak show and traveling circus or joining a seminary without clearly thinking it through.

After dealing with tremendous sunburns, an aching butt, a worn-out body, and fixing too many flat tires, I decided future adventures should require some basic research, not to say I was wholly against doing spur of the moment impulsive things. Like the time in the summer of 1968 when on a whim I decided to hitchhike from Los Angeles to New York to meet a stewardess girlfriend stationed in New York, but I'm getting ahead of myself and that's another story.

From September 1960 to June 1964, I attended a small and relatively new Bishop Alemany High School in Mission Hills, which was a Catholic high school next to San Fernando. The student population was comprised of a vast majority of whites, some Mexicans and two blacks.

I can honestly say that my high school years and where I lived covered a time of ambivalent racial tranquility, and the years were filled with good friends, great times, and an occasional social/racial screw-up.

In school, I was also successful playing different sports against all ethnicities across the Los Angeles area, and my high school exploits made me the proverbial "Big Man on Campus." To be honest, I figured my exciting life was a true blessing.

At the time, the racial tensions brewing in other parts of the U.S. seemed to be less of an issue in Southern California, and I frankly think it was because we all lived in a wonderland of beautiful beaches, Hollywood glamour, Disneyland, and an all-inclusive hippie culture which embraced a colorful ethnic utopia of Southern California Dreaming.

However, a brewing and unpopular war in Vietnam was also causing rebellious dissension among the younger generation of all colors. My young generation would naturally become cannon fodder for certain politicians, who supported democracy at all costs, especially the lucrative costs and profits collected by the military-industrial complex and shared with the corrupt elected officials.

Moreover, the newly signed Civil Rights Act of 1964 was stirring up social conflicts because of mandated racial job quotas and the bureaucratic bungling of overcorrecting unfair levels of living conditions of people of color. Suddenly, racial tensions began erupting in major cities all over America with blacks rioting against the establishment, demanding everything, and creating nasty police confrontations. Even California Dreaming was turning into a civic nightmare.

For me, I had left Southern California in 1964 for college in the placid state of Washington. I had won an academic/athlete scholarship in football at Washington State University (WSU), and I was now embracing a new and pleasant experience at a major west coast university that was inhabited by mostly law-abiding white students.

Of course, there was the obligatory number of out-of-state black student-athletes recruited by WSU for purposes of keeping up with their other opponents, who also knew the importance of having very athletic and super-fast blacks in their sports' programs and, fortunately, most of the black collegiate sports' stars had to semi-behave to stay in school.

My own WSU experience was abruptly ended by a neck injury in my first year, which prematurely terminated my football career due to the serious injury and an emotional breakdown brought on by the pressure of "failing" for the first time in my athletic career. I later gave my scholarship to a deserving student, even though I had an injury clause that allowed me to keep my scholarship, and sadly left for home in California.

After I arrived back in Southern California in late 1964, I realized that I had finally left the surreal comfort zone of being a sports and campus hero. I became traumatized by being unprepared and being thrust into a real world of struggling for identity and purpose and making excuses for failing and leaving an enviable college career.

In the ensuing months, I avoided friends and went back to school. I sought solace in living in San Fernando in my parents' spare bedroom, and the one redeeming benefit was that I kept my mom company while my dad was fighting for his life in the nearby Veteran's Hospital.

It seemed my dad's years of running his construction company and drinking a quart of Scotch whisky every night, followed by a half dozen aspirins for his morning hangover, finally caught up to him in his mid-forties and had virtually destroyed his entire stomach lining. It was rough visiting my ailing dad at the hospital and the first time he was able to talk to me, he found out about my early departure from WSU and just mumbled, "What the hell happened?"

Needless to say, that didn't help my bruised and battered emotional state and, to add salt and cayenne pepper to my wounds, I was further notified by my military draft board that my college deferment was terminated and to trade in my swimming trunks for camouflaged boxer shorts for Vietnam.

The following month, I had to report for my physical to begin the induction into Uncle Sam's military adventures overseas. Due to my current emotional state that was swirling around in a dirty toilet bowl, I actually remember feeling no qualms about going to Vietnam and getting my ass shot at in some godforsaken jungle. To be honest, being called up for military duty during a violent and screwed-up war created an unusual peace of mind for me. It was like knowing I was going to serve my country, which had been very good to me, even though the implementation of the controversial "Civil Rights and Screw Whitey Act of 1964," was a nagging issue for me, along with other personal setbacks that I brought on mostly by myself.

With the Vietnam war being unpopular in many corners of America and causing many ant-war demonstrations and social upheaval among the younger population in America, it was tempting for young American men to take an extended vacation to Canada as visiting tourist draft dodgers. For me, I didn't pass judgment on the Canadian vacationers and appeared one early sunny day for my military physical in downtown Los Angeles.

You talk about my being emotional in a swirling toilet, I encountered several guys who were already doing the backstroke down the sewer pipe at the military medical facility, which was entertaining hundreds of potential candidates for Vietnam cannon fodder. We felt like sheep being herded from one medical station to another for a quick check-and-next routine. I swear if you appeared before the eye doctor and had three eyes, he would probably say, "Interesting, but good, extra vision to kill more gooks, next in line!"

I was far removed from the time I took my college football scholarship physical in a nice facility with attentive nurses making sure I was comfortable and ready for the diligent doctor to report, "You look great. Now go out there and be eager to kick some ass for W.S.U., okay?"

During the military medical experience, there were guys selling pieces of aluminum foil for us to swallow, which they said would show up on the chest x-ray and possibly have some army private medic make a note that this guy's chest area has strange things inside. Another guy suddenly yelled, "I'm not going to fucking Nam," and he leaped right on top of a medical cart that carried a massive amount of urine specimens. Every urine vial and the soon-to-be detained protester went crashing to the floor.

In the aftermath, all the guys who had their urine donations decorating the floor had to give another sample. It was a tragic-comedic moment listening to the guys grunting and swearing, including me, who had just earlier drained our bladders and had to squeeze out another sample again.

I did make it to the final medical station and was half-heartedly asked by an older tired-looking doctor, "Any problems?" as a younger doctor was observing me and scanning my long medical questionnaire.

I replied "No," and was ordered to move ahead with several others toward a long green wall with large windows and two doors. Through the windows, I could see two waiting buses stationed at the two open doors. One door was marked "Army" with a pleasant-looking but unsmiling Army sergeant standing at the door's opening. The other door was marked "Marines" with a mean-looking and unsmiling Marine sergeant standing at the door's opening.

Needless to say, the line for the Army was quite long, whereas the line for the Marines was quite short.

However, in my longing to regain some of my demolished pride for blowing my "All American" career in college, I headed for the short Marines' line. You know the saying: "The Few. The Proud. The Marines." Or in my case, "The Semi-Proud Toilet Guy."

However, before I took even a few steps toward the Marine sergeant, who looked like he'd been to hell and back twice, I was pulled aside by a military staffer who returned me to the final medical station.

There, the younger military doctor who had earlier been studying my medical questionnaire, and who seemed more "dedicated" and more observant than the older doctor, was closely eyeballing my long questionnaire, which I had earlier filled out, and then began eyeballing me. He curtly asked me if I was playing games with the military with a possible debilitating medical condition.

Apparently, it had been a military problem that certain guys would lie about a hidden medical condition and later say it was caused by basic training, and then try to get discharged with some kind of benefits and military compensation.

The younger irritated doctor asked me why I said "No," when asked if I had any medical problems by the older doctor at the final station. He then pointed to my questionnaire where I had marked "Yes," where it asked if I have any serious allergy problems.

I replied that I didn't think it was that serious, so I said "No" to the older doctor. I was then accused of lying and was quickly escorted to a detention room, which also had the earlier urine cart leaper detained.

Finally, a military staffer came in the room and ordered me out of the facility, and that I would be called back in thirty to sixty days. I got a temporary military rejection card, and it was further ordered that when I returned that I was to bring back any medical records showing what allergies I had and how serious was my condition.

Great, I couldn't even get drafted and get my ass shot at in Vietnam, and now I would have to gather up old medical records and wait for an upcoming call to appear for another depressing military physical.

Moreover, after earlier playing rough sports like football and being in good shape, I had to now make up questionable excuses to people for my being unfit ("allergies?"), although most likely, I was just being disloyal for not joining the service for our country. I was sinking into a deeper abyss of a failed young man at such an early age, and Canada was looking better all the time.

However, after waiting several months for my military call back and languishing in self-pity and the beginnings of alcoholism, I began to wonder if there was a cosmic conspiracy to fuck with me for my past digressions and denigrating the hallowed "Civil Rights Act of 1964," which created the "Great American Payback to White Privileged Assholes."

Meanwhile, a radical anti-war organization called the Weathermen or something, blew up a section of the military records facility that kept the draft status records of the young men in the area where I lived.

Much later after the Vietnam War ended in 1973 as a result of the Paris peace accord, I found out the blast obliterated the records of guys with last names beginning with "A" to "D." So, my charred records were probably classified as missing in a domestic terrorist action. I never heard from the military selective service board again. I guess I did figuratively experience Vietnam era combat with my records and picture being bombed into kingdom come by Vietcong wannabes.

Back to the spring of 1965, I still rejected the idea of returning to school, but I finally decided to come out of hiding and got a low-paying menial job at the nearby San Fernando Park. It was a decent job, and I oversaw the recreational activities of people enjoying the various opportunities to have picnics, play baseball, tennis, basketball, ping pong, etc. The park visitors were a combination of whites, Mexicans, and several blacks from Pacoima that didn't have a recreational park at the time.

The racial interactions were mostly peaceful, except for an occasional minor ruckus between the blacks and Mexicans over picnic areas. I did my best to create racial harmony in the park and I would break the park rules to achieve peaceful coexistence of the different tribes, e.g., 1) I made deals with the Mexicans and blacks to which areas they could claim as their turf; 2) I kept the black guys busy with free checkouts of balls and equipment; 3) I even let the black guys play tackle football that was forbidden in the park, and I even joined in on occasion to their delight in gang tackling a white guy; 4) I let the black teenage girls and older women fight because any white guy is a fool to try and break up a fight between black girls (which I learned from black guys); and 5) I also left the lights on in certain "closed" areas of the park at night for the blacks to play cards, drink, etc.

This type of park supervision made me friends with the different ethnic leaders, especially with "Tank," a gigantic black guy who seemed to rule the black brothers.

But my attempts to stay on the good side of the brothers did meet with disapproval from my white prick of a boss, who never had to deal with the mostly unemployed brothers and just kept warning me about being fired. Maybe I should have told Tank that my boss was a ranking member of the Klu Klux Klan and given him my boss's home address.

Unfortunately, the park's mostly tranquil activities all changed when the infamous Los Angeles Watts Riots broke out in the summer of 1965.

The riots started when an upstanding young black gang member and high school dropout named Marquette "borrowed" his mother's 1955 Buick and was pulled over for drunk driving in a city called Watts, which was located in impoverished south central L.A. His brother immediately got out of the car, ran a few blocks home, and notified their mother about Marquette's predicament.

Well, Mama came running back with Marquette's brother and gave Marquette a black-mama scolding about taking her fine-looking Buick and driving around drunk.

Meanwhile, the white California Highway Patrolman (CHP) tried to intervene—(remember the earlier advice about being a white guy and not interfering when pissed-off black people are fighting amongst themselves)—well, all hell broke loose when CHP Lee M. jumped in and Marquette, his brother, and his mama began directing their agitation toward a lone CHP officer, who quickly became very outnumbered when over two hundred other civic-minded black people started throwing rocks and yelling, "Whitey is beating up an old black lady!"

So began the Watts Riots of 1965, which lasted about a week and spilled over to neighboring L.A. cities and towns, including Pacoima and part of San Fernando.

During all this chaos, the black Pacoima rioters chose San Fernando Park as a meeting place. They wrote a letter to the San Fernando city fathers and demanded the park be closed to all non-black outsiders, except one token white guy worker, who would still check out basketballs and footballs, and turn on the lights at night. Incredibly, the nervous white city fathers agreed, not wanting to escalate a very dangerous situation, and chose a white hostage worker to comply with the brothers' wishes.

Every evening, the brothers lit bonfires in the park, shot their guns in the air, and chanted: "Down with the white people!" Then they would head out to riot and loot in the surrounding areas.

Fortunately for that one white park worker, Tank had approached him and said everything was cool with him because he had been okay with the brothers prior to the riots. The brothers did enjoy firing their guns near his office late at night to make his asshole pucker up, but the worker did survive his very unusual tour of park duty.

I should know, I was that half-crazy and half-cowering white worker who gained some "street cred" in dealing with pissed-off and crazy black rioters, who considered me just as crazy, although semi-gutsy, in still checking out basketballs to the brothers after returning back from the riots at night and playing hoops wearing stolen tuxedos and brand-new Converse black basketball shoes. Furthermore, after being rejected by the military to fight in Vietnam, I felt I was gaining some combat glory right in the middle of San Fernando Park, although I didn't get any extra combat pay. Like I said earlier, I worked for a real prick of a cheap-ass boss.

There was a major highlight for me in the fall of 1965 when my older brother Don was head water boy for the Los Angeles Rams. My brother was a great baseball player and had signed with the Los Angeles Dodgers for the 1965 spring training camp in Vero Beach, Florida, He had a serious injury at the end of spring training that cut his baseball career short and he was bouncing around Los Angeles doing various activities after his short baseball stint in Vero Beach.

He would visit me at the San Fernando Park where the Los Angeles Rams used the large baseball facilities for summer training in 1965.

My brother got to know the Rams players and coaches and he agreed to work all the Sunday home games for the Rams in the Los Angeles Coliseum, and he picked me as his assistant water boy. What a great and fun experience to be a small part of the National Football League (NFL) and meet several of the great stars from that era. Thinking back, I believe my beloved brother, who at the time I didn't realize was battling his own demons and severe white guilt over race issues, wanted me to experience the thrill of being on the NFL field and feel the excitement of being a part of the game of football again, which became an uplifting panacea after my miserable football downfall at Washington State University and the traumatic experience of earlier dealing with the dangerous Watts Riots at the San Fernando Park.

My domestic tour of combat duty at the park lasted until New Year's Day in 1966. I was still living at home helping my mom and I had enough money to survive a spell without a job. I bought a used Honda 250 Scrambler motorcycle and decided to take short road trips to expand my life experiences. It didn't take long for me to experience a surreal road experience when a drunk driver, who was racing down the road in front of my parents' house, struck me broadside as I was pulling into our driveway around midnight.

It was a freakish horrific accident, as I was launched into the neighbor's front patio and the car hurtled through the air upside down and landed on top of me. The car caused an explosion of broken wood and plaster, and I somehow survived and laid face up and semi-conscious under the car's roof with my head and left arm sticking out near the driver's window. The explosion of white plaster dust swirled around me, and in my dazed condition, I thought, "This is it, I died and I'm headed up through the white clouds to heaven."

This moment of peace, dying with no pain and ascending into heaven just like the Catholic priests told me, was suddenly interrupted by my friendly neighbor, Mr. Martinez, who rushed out from inside his damaged house to see what the hell exploded into the front of his house. He was yelling in Spanish at his wife and in my state of diminished comprehension from the crash and my biased upbringing in the Catholic Church by white priests made me say to myself, "Hey, they don't speak Spanish in heaven." I was now slightly more lucid about my still ongoing existence on earth. I was also pissed that I had to experience death again later in life. What a bummer.

The next thing Mr. Martinez did was to step near the driver's window to help pull out the inebriated and mostly unhurt driver. I guess it's true that if you're drunk in a bad accident, you drunkenly fly around without really hurting yourself too much.

Since the porch light got obliterated in the crash, Mr. Martinez was struggling in the dark to assist the idiot driver, who just helped me to set a new personal record of flying through space. In the rush to help the driver, Mr. Martinez had inadvertently stepped on my face. He was unaware of my being trapped under the car in the dark and covered in crash debris. I winced in pain and struggled to reach up and grabbed a startled Mr. Martinez by the throat with my free left hand, gasping, "Mr. Martinez, you're, you're stepping on my face!"

By this time, Mr. Martinez had gotten a flashlight from his wife and shined it toward the sound of my voice under the debris, which I had moved partially out of the way with my free injured left hand. Telling the car's driver to hold on for a minute, Mr. Martinez leaned down closer to me, winced at my bloodied face, and began to faint. Quickly, Mrs. Martinez grabbed Mr. Martinez and got the flashlight and she shined the light down toward the bizarre scene of my spitting out blood and debris. Then she hysterically yelled for her sons to come help.

As the very strong Martinez sons, who were all weightlifters, ran over to help lift the car off me, I heard the driver complain about his not being helped out first. I remembered succinctly saying to the driver, "Fuck you."

Four weeks later, after spending two earlier weeks in the hospital, I was resting on my parents' front porch in a reinforced lounge chair that my mom had rigged in such a way that I would be secure. I was still encased in a 75 percent size body cast to let my traumatized body and broken bones slowly heal in peace.

As I squirmed in my heavy plaster pajamas, my friend Louie stopped by riding a used Honda 250 Scrambler motorcycle, which he had rebuilt using the engine from my totally destroyed 250. I had vaguely remembered that Louie visited me in the hospital and asked me when I was in a fog of painkillers, "Hey, I saw your demolished 250 and only the engine seemed to be undamaged. Can I use it to rebuild my 250?"

I hesitated at the tragic-comedic question of could I let Louie have my engine since my 250 and I were in no condition to go riding for quite some time, if ever? I finally replied, "Sure, Louie, the engine is all yours."

Well, the day that Louie stopped by to see me, he had a special purpose and a plan that he had put together. He had attached supports and gadgets to the back of his 250, which would hold me in place for a ride around town. Louie reminded me of the old saying that if you get bucked off a horse, you got to get back on or you'll never ride again.

I agreed, and after having my complete left leg cast tied to the side of Louie's 250 and my bandaged right leg secured to the other side, and my upper body cast that was hinged at the waist and fully secured with straps to the bike seat, I used my only partially free left limb and hand to hold onto the collar of Louie's coat. My mom, a tough and understanding Norwegian, who had come outside to check on what I was doing, just shook her head and waved bye as we headed for Louie's house.

About fifteen minutes as we headed to Pacoima where Louie lived, a wailing siren forced Louie to pull over on the side of the highway.

I thought Louie pulled over to let an ambulance pass by, as I couldn't turn around to see what was happening. But Louie told me the cops had just pulled us over. I could hear car doors opening and closing from behind, and Louie got off the 250 and steadied the bike on the kickstand, while I teetered and wobbled around with only my left hand holding onto the seat strap.

Eventually looking to my right, I strained to see a befuddled police officer grabbing my wobbling body, looking at me, and asking, "What the hell are you trying to do, kill yourself?" He then looked over at Louie and barked, "Would you mind explaining this? Your friend's in a body cast strapped to your damn motorcycle and you were doing over 50 miles an hour!"

I jumped in to help Louie, telling the officer it was my idea and that I needed to get out of the house and go riding for therapy. The cop studied me for a moment and frowned, asking me in a curious manner, "Tell me, how did you end up in the body cast?"

While I was trying to gather my thoughts about explaining to a concerned cop about my unique accident, Louie piped in, "He was in a bad motorcycle accident."

The cop stared at Louie, then he placed his hand on my body cast and looked me in the eye, inquiring, "Is that really true?" I nodded in the affirmative.

He turned back to his partner, who was monitoring police calls by the police car's front door, and yelled back to him, "Hey, you wanna know *why* this guy strapped on the back of this motorcycle is in a body cast?"

The cop's partner yelled back over the noise of the busy highway traffic, "Why?"

The cop next to me shouted back to his partner, "He was in a fucking motorcycle accident!"

After minutes of discussion and some strained laughter at the amateur attempt of motorcycle therapy for me, the officers unstrapped me and slowly and awkwardly placed me in the back of their police car. They proceeded to follow Louie to his house and, after convincing Louie's mom that she should drive me back to my home in their family car, they didn't even write a citation for Louie and his accomplice for the reckless endangerment of a loon encased in body plaster. The cops just chalked it up to young guys and their fearless but somewhat dumb bravado.

One month later, I was completely out of my three-quarter body cast and began rehabbing my battered and bruised body.

After several weeks, my great mom helped me feel better and encouraged me to tackle life's adventures and misadventures again. I received some insurance money and started to do challenging endeavors to build up my confidence. I trained and received both my private pilot's license and SCUBA diving card. These activities didn't involve racial affirmative action—sharks will bite your ass whether you're black or white—and if you screw up a landing, mother earth will not check your ethnicity before you augur into a big hole.

I also went to work at the Standard Stations Company, which had several company gas stations in the surrounding Los Angeles area.

I was assigned to work at Station 1844, which was located close to my parents' house, and was on a major highway between Mission Hills and Granada Hills. Our customers were mostly white people living in the area and various travelers on vacation or business. The pay was just above minimum wage, but we all got free gas for our vehicles when one of our workers discovered how to change the price to "zero" per gallon of gas.

It was the summertime of 1966 and my brother Don, who was attending UCLA at the time, visited me at the gas station and convinced me to enroll back in college.

So, in the fall of 1966, I enrolled as an older freshman at California State University at Northridge and continued to work full-time at Station 1844 at night. It was a grind going back to college and working at night, but I realized it made my family and friends glad to see me trying to academically and personally forge ahead.

I even tried out and made the freshman basketball team and enjoyed the college competition again. At 6'2" I was too slow for a guard, and somewhat short for a forward in those days of college basketball, which emphasized certain racial speed and athletic ability to jump over the basketball rim.

In other words, college basketball was beginning to mostly become a sport for black athletes, but I did make the team and became the "sixth man" player, who substituted to relieve the starting forwards. I even had the opportunity to play against the famous UCLA freshmen team, which had an unbelievable star athlete by the name of Lew Alcindor—later named Kareem Abdul-Jabbar—when he was a Hall of Fame basketball player for the Los Angeles Lakers.

Frankly, in those early days of athletics, I didn't mind seeing the blacks excel in various sports, which were based on abilities. But in the more serious arena of the job place, I was getting bummed out by the affirmative action policies that favored people of color, who had fewer abilities than their white counterparts.

The reverse discrimination against whites got me rejected by both the Los Angeles Police Department (LAPD) and L.A. Fire Department (LAFD), due to minority racial quotas to be filled before whites would be hired.

Like several young white boys growing up, I had dreams of being a sports hero, or a hero policeman or fireman someday. Granted, some whites, who got public employment points for military service, did get hired during my attempt to join the LAPD.

In 1967, I witnessed this affirmative action (racial discrimination based on color and not merit) firsthand when I made it through all the LAPD pre-screening medicals, physical tests, and interviews. I also had several recommendations from friendly and supportive LAPD motorcycle cops who filled up their gas tanks at Station 1844.

At my last LAPD interview, it was explained to me that although I was one of the top three candidates, who were all white guys, only one white was selected for the three open positions due to his previous military experience. The other two selectees were both black guys who were nice and friendly, but I was still upset and realized that my domestic "combat experience" at the San Fernando Park wouldn't give me any needed points to get fucking hired.

These disappointments at the LAPD and the LAFD, and the tedious school and work grind, were starting to wear me down. It caused me to lose spirit, and I wasn't that all-together mentally from all the racial quota rejections and previous physical traumas that I had suffered.

In a spontaneous move, I quit my job at Station 1844 and hitchhiked to New York to follow TV host Art Linkletter's television advice and to see America firsthand for motivation to be successful. Furthermore, my new girlfriend had just been transferred to New York as an airline stewardess and had invited me to visit her. I did make it, but we broke up shortly after I arrived, due to my being broke, my moodiness, and rules against my living in a stew zoo (company housing for the stewardesses). So, I headed back home.

Luckily, my supportive parents helped bail me out of this challenging time of frustration and growing anxiety. They assisted me financially when I wanted to leave L.A. and desired to attend the very popular San Diego State University in the fall of 1968.

For the record, I really enjoyed the next two years in laidback San Diego, even after a chaotic start in my renewed academic career.

The chaos started when being an older transfer student, my first-semester registration was scheduled for the afternoon of the very last day. I think there were about six classes left open, e.g., History of Outer Mongolia, The Brilliance of Andy Warhol's Underwear Drawings, and Theater Costume and Makeup, which were among the few. I signed up for Costume and Makeup and had to crash my other three courses to fill my full semester schedule.

One was my required English class where I sat on the floor for two weeks before the irritated teacher finally relented and said if I found a chair, she would sign my registration form. I immediately got up and went down the hallway and found a graduate math class in The Relationship of Molecular Models and Advanced Calculus or something. How could this class be possibly filled? So, I entered the classroom on an emergency chair procurement mission and saw only one empty chair in a class full of super math nerds and a teacher who just stared at me. I picked up the chair and asked to borrow it. The seventy-six year-old teacher just nodded and I was on my way.

My other two classes were in the dramatic arts department. One class was Set and Scenery Construction and the other was a Stage Management course. These classes involved blending in with theater types and keeping busy, and the instructors seemed oblivious to my presence. I eventually had teacher assistants sign my registration forms to officially enter the class, saying I had forgotten to have them signed earlier.

Ironically, I had entered into a major course of study that seemed surreal to me, but it eventually proved to be a blessing in disguise. Even though I played rough and tough sports in front of large crowds of people, I was terribly insecure in speaking in front of people in any class and other situations, and I truly suffered from "stage fright." I somehow had the school registration department officially enter my major as Communication Arts (later called Dramatic Arts), or as I called my major "Traumatic Arts." I never even used a counselor and scribbled a counselor's name on my registration form, which was required but never really checked by the pimple-faced freshmen registration helpers who worked as student workers in the school's registration department.

My first year was a blast, except when I had to prepare scenes in my early acting classes. I could memorize lines but was extremely nervous and mumbled too much.

One day, an instructor finally stopped my oral delivery in a scene and asked me, "What is your problem with articulation and projection?"

I responded that I was really nervous, and he stopped everything and announced he needed to help me with trust in myself and others. I was six foot and two inches tall, and he instructed me to stretch out on the floor face up. Then the whole class followed his instructions to pick me up and carry me around the stage above their heads. There were a few groans about lifting me up, but I was slowly raised up and the instructor told me to let go and trust I wouldn't be dropped. He further instructed me to say my lines up to the ceiling with confidence and feeling.

Damn, it was a true awakening. I spoke my lines with gusto and went limp in my classmates' supportive arms and hands. Everyone cheered my breakthrough, and I felt such an overall release of tension that I accidentally farted real long and loud and we all fell into a heap of laughter and coughing.

My next breakout performance occurred during the summer school vacation of 1969. I qualified for a student trip to Cambridge University in England to attend summer courses in English literature and poetry. I did so well that I didn't even have to pay for the trip. I was used in several promotional shots for the student tour company and the company waived my trip fees.

In my final year beginning in the fall of 1969, I was interested in a U.S. Navy recruitment booth on campus. The controversial Vietnam War was still a turbulent social issue in America, and I witnessed the Navy recruiter receiving abuse and name-calling from radical anti-war students.

On a day off from classes, I sat down and talked to the recruiter, and I explained my earlier hectic time with the military. After filling out some applications, he said he would enter me into a college NAVROC (like ROTC for the Army) program. I took the military aptitude test and aced it. He then encouraged me to graduate soon by June of 1970 because he had only a few slots for officer's pilot training. Things were looking up and I started figuring out what courses I needed to graduate by the following June. I also received an insurance settlement from my motorcycle accident and bought a used 1964 Corvette Stingray coupe with a gigantic 427 horsepower engine. It greatly helped my transportation needs since some juvenile delinquent black bastard from our on-campus mentoring program for troubled youths in the area stole my Schwinn bicycle. I even forgave the little bastard after catching him on campus riding my bike, telling him I didn't need the old bike since the Good Lord graciously traded it up for me in the transportation department with a cool set of wheels that had an engine, too! I was frankly getting tired of riding my bike all over San Diego and it had cramped my dating opportunities, too.

While contemplating my future "Chuck Yeager" fighter pilot escapades, I noticed a promotional flyer on my dorm's bulletin board. The flyer's title read: "Want a thrill? Try Parachuting!" Wow, that sounded great. I could learn how to parachute to add to my pre-military private flying experience. The only problem was I was short on money for extracurricular activities, even fuel for my gas-guzzling Corvette. I then read below the parachuting flyer about a part-time job opening as a receptionist at a large mortuary/cemetery five miles east of downtown San Diego. It was called Greenwood Memorial Park and Mortuary and it covered a whopping 125 acres. It was advertised as the largest and busiest mortuary and cemetery in San Diego, and it boasted that it had twenty-two visitation rooms. The contact person for the part-time job was a guy living in my dorm and I went to his room for more details. He said that he currently held the job but needed to quit. The mortuary said it would give him a parting bonus if he could find a replacement before he quit. All his replacement needed was a dark suit and show up on time (5pm to 9pm) to the reception area for the constantly filled twenty-two viewing rooms. The receptionist just had to guide the bereaved family and friends to the rooms of their dearly departed. It was daily with the weekends off, and it sounded like an easy way to make some extra bucks for parachuting and dating, and not be a strain on my scholarly pursuits.

Since for some odd reason I was the only guy with a dark suit in the dorm who had inquired about the mortuary receptionist position, I was the lucky winner of a job that I soon discovered was very strange after working a few nights at the creepy place.

The following bizarre episodes happened during my unusual occupation at the Greenwood Memorial Park and Spook Show:

The Night Mortician's Tacos

After clocking in, one of my first tasks was to check with the night mortician for the list of the deceased and their room numbers in order to respectfully guide the grieving visitors to the correct rooms. One particular evening when I checked on the night mortician, who was kind of a slob and oblivious to all the dead bodies all over his workplace, he was happily munching on his favorite Jack in the Box tacos while dripping taco sauce from his chin and draining a dead body of its fluids and infusing taco sauce and formaldehyde into its system. I had to hold back the urge to vomit, even more so when he offered me some tacos that were stashed in the fridge containing creepy body parts kept in jars for possible forensic examinations. On certain occasions when I would pick up a body at an area hospital to bring back to Greenwood, the night mortician would ask me to stop at a Jack in the Box for some tacos. You can already guess the jokes I heard from the drive-through attendants when I pulled up to the take-out window in a Greenwood hearse with a coffin in the back. "Hey, who's in the box, Jack?" I can still remember the sight of the taco sauce dripping from the night mortician's mouth and onto the body he was working on below him on the drain table.

Spooky Inspections

Part of my job was inspecting the visitation rooms before viewing hours as the wind whistled through the eerie and dimly lit long corridors. The large windows were kept open, which provided ventilation to lower the pungent odor of mortuary smells, and the moving drapes and curtains added to the eeriness and my jumpiness. On a particularly windy night, one of our horizontal guests was a well-known and stunning San Diego stripper who had been murdered by a jealous boyfriend, and she was resting in eternal repose in one of our visitation rooms at the end of a long, dark windy corridor. A young black stripper begged me to follow her all the way to the room to pay her respects, but I had an emergency and led her to the start of the corridor and told her to just walk all the way to the end and enter the last room on the left. I guess she made it about halfway when I heard the crash of a flashlight bouncing down the corridor and she let out a blood-curdling scream and fled out the front door. Later, when I inspected what all the commotion was about, I discovered that the flashlight-throwing culprit was our resident practical joker and fat-ass white security guard, who had damn near woke up some of our other resting souls with all the racket.

Winking Dead Bodies

During my first few weeks at Greenwood, I would double-check some bodies that I swore would twitch and wink at me in my nervous state of mind. Greenwood had very talented makeup artists, who could make dead people seem so life-like it was downright nerve-wracking for a college student just trying to earn a few bucks for sky-diving lessons. My favorite makeup artist was an older lady who always dressed in Gothic black gowns and wore creepy black and white makeup. If you spoke to her, she would just smile and return to the body she was working on and spoke to the dead person. I guess she preferred speaking with the dead more than speaking to real live people. Maybe it prevented awkward conversations for her.

The Statue Lady

During my first time taking a security stroll through the beautiful gravesites and some creepy monuments at night, I approached the infamous "Statue Lady." I wasn't yet aware of all the ghoulish details of the white figurine and when I got close to the weird-looking statue in a kneeling position with its head down in a dark part of the cemetery, I swore the statue moved. I got closer and the statue's head suddenly popped up and it/she loudly yelled at me to not disturb her husband. I jumped back and quickly ran through the cemetery to the safety of my office.

The night guard laughed his fat ass off when I told him what I saw, and then he joked that he knew about the "Statue Lady" and had nefariously set me up and sent me to the area to check on the cemetery grounds and any graffiti on the statues since he had faked a sprained ankle. The fat-ass guard said he "forgot" to tell me about the fucking statue weirdo, who was a very disturbed naked lady who painted herself in all white. There were no night visitors allowed in the cemetery area, so she would catatonically pose with other statues next to her deceased husband. Apparently, she was very wealthy and the mortuary management would allow her to grieve since she paid big bucks for all the statues and fancy gravesite for her dead husband. I promised the guard I would get revenge on him somehow in the future, but then we both laughed at my almost crapping in my pants.

Mexican Priests Don't Like Ramblers

It was interesting although sometimes very stressful dealing with the contrasting groups of bereaved people who would gather for memorial services in our mourning chapel. For example, it was nearly impossible when I attempted to calm down an irate gathering of Mexican mourners because their stubborn and delayed Mexican priest, who was about seven miles away from Greenwood at their parish church in south Chula Vista. He refused to be picked up in our tacky Rambler station wagon that was used for our less prominent VIP memorial ministers. One of the more violent mourners had called the priest who complained about the racist Greenwood management and their apparent refusal to pick him up in one our beautiful Cadillacs.

It was a fact that the owner of Greenwood at the time also own a car dealership that sold Ramblers and Cadillacs, and we had a small fleet of the tacky Rambler vehicles used for tacky transportation needs, like picking up a Mexican priest from Chula Vista. Greenwood naturally reserved the beautiful black Cadillacs for our more prominent VIPs.

So, I was in the middle of a Mexican revolution at the mourning chapel, and I wasn't allowed to use the Caddies unless I had special permission. What the hell? I figured the Mexican priest wouldn't mind being chauffeured in my cool blue Corvette Stingray and I told the Mexican mourners to be patient and that their beloved priest would be arriving soon. I rushed into the mortician's room and told the on-duty mortician I had to leave on a mercy mission and asked him to watch the reception area and the chapel. He wasn't busy at the time but still groaned at my request. He then suggested, "Why don't you wear the spare priest outfit that's stored in our clothes closet?' The clothes closet was used for storing outfits for our "permanent" customers waiting to be placed in their respective dirt beds. But one sporty priest, who would leave from the golf course in his golfing clothes to attend a memorial service, would keep his priest outfit in our closet ready for his Greenwood appearance. I declined the suggestion, knowing the Mexican mourning mob would have a fit seeing a fake white guy priest, pretending he was a part-time minister and also the goofy Greenwood receptionist. Twenty minutes later, I dropped off a semi-dazed Mexican priest, who agreed to ride in my Vette that had gone nearly supersonic during our "Fast & Furious" ride to Greenwood. He actually thanked me for the unusual but thrilling Greenwood transportation ride. Although later, I received a management warning letter to *not* use my car for Greenwood Memorial transportation needs.

In contrast to the tense Mexican service, the other much different memorial service in which I assisted was a beautiful and serendipitous "mourning" event held by a group of very happy people, who didn't have a minister or a priest. They had moved to San Diego from the South Pacific islands and were celebrating the passing of one of their relatives into that big, beautiful island in the sky. I was even invited to a luau they prepared outdoors in a Greenwood patio reception area.

What a different memorial mood than the Mexican group, which even had a few rowdy gang members in attendance. The Mexicans followed their respectful mourning rites with very somber actions and occasional wailing from a distraught relative, which I did truly respect. But I have to say the luau was great.

"Where's My Harry?!"

One slow night when I was relaxing in my reception office and reading a Playboy magazine, a large white woman burst into my small reception office through the open side door and grabbed my throat from behind, screaming, 'Where's my Harry?!" Luckily, the security guard was close by and came in to lift the lady off me after we had fallen to the floor.

After catching my breath, I hysterically asked, "What the hell you talking about, lady?!" She said her husband was not in his room. So, the security guard, the lady, and I went to check on the problem. I quickly observed that Harry's name card was clearly inserted in the door's card holder and we all entered the room. We all gazed at an old white woman peacefully placed in a simple casket. The guard looked at me and winked. The guard then told the lady to wait outside while we fixed the situation. The guard closed and locked the door and told me to check the closet. Lo and behold, there was Harry, propped up in the closet with flowers and a nice wreath, saying, "Bye Harry," hanging on his head.

The guard and I quickly did a switcheroo with Harry and the deceased old lady, and then we opened the door and invited the large lady to visit her dearly departed husband. She seemed dazed at the sudden appearance of her Harry, but the guard and I quickly made our exit to stop her from asking any questions about where the other body went. The guard then laughed and told me that the new young mortician screwed up and didn't tell me that we were short one room that night. The new mortician should have advised me to notify him to switch the bodies with the guard's help, while I would delay the visitor if she or he was seeing Harry or the deceased old lady.

I didn't laugh and went back to the mortician's area and found the young mortician reading a car dealership pamphlet for a beautiful Porsche. He had just bought a new yellow Porsche and asked if I wanted to see it in the parking lot. I said, "Hell no, and fucking warn me about any switched bodies in the future!" He then chuckled and said the guard had just called him about the mix-up with Harry. I gave him the finger and left, thinking how I would retaliate against the smart-ass young mortician with a new Porsche.

Free Aromatic Dating Flowers

While working at Greenwood, I did save money on my college dates with free flowers, which I had confiscated from the leftover bouquets at the mortuary trash bins.

However, some of my more astute dates knew that I worked at Greenwood, and they would comment on the lovely smell of the mortuary and the formaldehyde aroma emanating from their unusually scented floral gift. They also knew about my lack of date money and would just laugh at my bizarre dating etiquette.

Last Night at Greenwood and PLFs

I had left early on my last night working at Greenwood and when I approached the young mortician's covered Porsche in the parking lot, I lifted up the front part of the cover and spray-painted in big red letters VW on the yellow hood. "VW" stood for Volkswagen, which was a joke German car to snooty Porsche owners. Revenge is mine, sayeth the Lord, and also for other people, too.

After getting my last two paychecks at Greenwood, I did venture over to a dirt airstrip several miles from school and signed up for my parachute training. It was an experience I would never forget.

An ex-military parachute jumper nicknamed "Stretch" was our jumpmaster. We had a group of five fearless souls who were daring to conquer the skies and for whatever reason jump out of a perfectly operating airplane thousands of feet in the air.

After finishing our ground school and practicing PLFs (Parachute Landing Falls), we got outfitted in our surplus military-type parachutes.

Initial parachute jumps are done with a static line connected to the airplane—to prevent the possibility of a rookie forgetting to pull his/her rip cord and go splat—and then after the static line automatically pulled out the rip cord and parachute, you would gently float to Mother Earth in your used military surplus chute and hopefully perform a proper PLF to prevent breaking both of your damn ankles.

The static line chute we used was different than a "skydiving" chute, which is used in free falls. Most skydiving chutes have fancy designs and pull cords that guide your actions while descending to a precise location for a standing landing.

After being outfitted in our chutes and given last minute instructions, we were boarded into an old but trustworthy single-engine, high-wing airplane with a large exit door near the right wing.

When we reached our jump altitude and near our ground target area, Stretch called for me to be the first to lead the way. I hooked up my static line, climbed out the door, and stood on a wing strut while holding onto an upper strut. We were told to just push off from the upper strut and sail away. As I stood on the strut I heard Stretch yell at the others to observe what I was doing. He then yelled out to me about remembering what steps to do, e.g., after the initial jolt of releasing from the plane, you'll feel a tug from the chute opening and you need to look up to observe a full open canopy and not a twisted streamer or no open canopy, after which you would then have to deploy your emergency chute.

After Stretch had yelled at me, "Did I remember all my steps?" I yelled back in anxious anticipation of leaping from a perfectly good flying airplane, "I don't remember a fucking thing!" I then let go and what a rush. Next was a tug and I was anxiously looking up and relieved that I had a full open chute.

Following my thanking the Good Lord for my open canopy, I encountered the most strange and quiet environment I had ever experienced. I was totally mesmerized by the beauty of the vast open sky and the absolute silence.

My standard chute did have simple pull chords to turn the chute for directional movements into or against the wind to guide yourself to your landing area. As I descended, I was singing and actually wished I could jerk off. I also remembered Stretch instructing us to observe when things got bigger on the ground below because that meant you were getting close to the ground and you needed to prepare yourself for hitting the ground with a well-executed PLF and not a poorly-executed splat on Mother Earth.

Unfortunately, in my landing scenario, Stretch later said he accidentally misjudged the quirky winds on my jump. Consequently, I ended up a hundred yards or so from the clear landing area and I landed in a ravine full of large rocks and thorny bushes. I haphazardly did an unusual PLF to miss landing in a large bush and ended up on my ass while straddling another thorny bush inches away from my pecker.

After carefully extracting myself away from the menacing thorny bush, I gathered my chute and jogged back to the airstrip and stood on the runway, preventing the airplane and Stretch from landing in protest over my near scrotum disaster. But Stretch was a cool customer and just put on his free-fall chute and landed right outside his office trailer door.

When I finally reached the office, he was grinning and handed my personal jump logbook to me. He had written in the comments section of my first logged jump: "Good exit, kicking and waving on way down. Rough landing in a rocky ravine due to reasons beyond jumper's control." Like I said, Stretch was a cool dude. But I did tell him that due to his slight misjudgment, I almost had my second circumcision by doing a half-ass PLF into a big thorny bush.

To celebrate my cheating death and successfully surviving the slight miscue of a lighthearted and good jumpmaster, I stopped at my favorite hamburger joint and had a big Whopper. I then proceeded to the movie theater and watched "Paint Your Wagon." It was a fun movie and I got a kick out of hearing tough guy actor Lee Marvin sing.

Later that night, I went to a nightclub on Shelter Island to hear my cousin play drums in a rock and roll band at a very popular night spot. I was sitting on a stool near the dance floor when over all the music and noise, I heard a very distinctive voice behind me. I turned around and sitting at a table nearby was one of my favorite actors and the "famous singer" in "Paint Your Wagon." Lee Fucking Marvin!

I walked over to Marvin's table as he was talking to two guys in suits. He was in his tennis attire and seemed bored with the business talk going on. I waited for a good time to interrupt and said to Marvin that I enjoyed his movie 'Paint Your Wagon" and even liked his singing. He laughed and exclaimed, "Damn, thank you, but that singing scared the hell out of me!"

Meanwhile, the two suits just stared at me for a moment and asked me to leave and not bother Mr. Marvin. Marvin seemed annoyed at the two suits and told them to leave and invited me to sit and have a drink with him. I guess he wanted to talk to a regular person and just relax and drink. We had a few drinks and I can truthfully say that Marvin was a great guy and enjoyed basic bullshitting with one of his fans, whom he treated like a friend.

I told him I was studying dramatic arts at San Diego State, and he didn't mind my asking what it took to make it in the movies as an actor, writer, etc. He told me to believe in yourself and whatever they give you, take it and run with it, even blow it up a bit to get some positive attention. I then related to him I had watched a previous small movie scene that he had in a jail cell, where he gyrated and struggled with his jail keepers, shouting and making "a scene." I also told him that I had seen him on TV making fun of his movie death scenes, where he takes extra time to dramatically die. Marvin laughed at my recollections and reminded me to enjoy the movie business if I get the chance to be a part of it.

Before we parted company, I told him I preferred the writing side of movies and he bought me a last drink and wryly said, "Good luck, there are several million writers who also want your job."

Much later in life, I made a trip to Arlington National Cemetery to pay my respects to all the veterans who had served, including paying special thanks to a great guy, successful actor, and respected member of the U.S. Marines. RIP Lee Marvin.

In my final spring semester in 1970, I ended up registering for 27 credits (15 credits were a full semester load) and requested another three credits by writing a paper for my summer courses in England. This was all approved by the university's president with whom I met and explained that I wanted to join the military and needed his approval for the multiple credit overload. To sway the president's decision, I think the president was pleased with my wanting to leave school and join the military since during our meeting, there were several Vietnam War student protestors sitting and yelling outside his door about allowing military recruiters on campus. They were also longtime "professional" students who refused to leave from the president's office area until he came out and spoke to them. When I came out I smiled and said the president says, "Hello, have a nice day."

Wow! What a semester I had scheduled. A full year's academic work of thirty credits in one semester. The big question was could I pull it off?

Halfway through the semester, I was so busy with papers, tests, projects, etc., I started losing my sense of direction and sanity. Was it all worth it to finish this madness to join the U.S. Navy and get my ass shot down over the friendly jungles of Vietnam?

Fortunately, it was a week before Easter Break at San Diego State U., and a dorm roommate at school was singing in the bathroom before our morning classes, "Mazatlan, Mazatlan, here I come, man, Mazatlan!"

I stopped his singing and asked, "What's this Mazatlan thing you're singing about?" He told me that college students from the southwestern parts of the United States (Arizona, New Mexico, San Diego, etc.) would all meet at the Mexican border town of Mexicali, which is right across the border from Calexico, California. The Mexican railway system set up extra passenger cars for a special Easter Break train trip to Mazatlan, Mexico, which was on the Pacific coast across from the southernmost tip of Baja, California, and was known for its outrageous spring breaks for crazy rich Americano and Americana college students.

Needing a serious break from my overloaded schedule and my overloaded brain cells, I pleaded, "Where do I sign up?"

After getting a quick tourist visa and advising my family and friends I was going to Mexico for Easter Break, I left with my roommate and two other students and drove from San Diego to Calexico. We safely parked the car in California and crossed the border to Mexicali, Mexico. The train fare was cheap for the 1000-mile (25-hour) trip and all the rail cars were packed like sardines with student bodies all over the place. Students were crammed in the seats, in the overhead luggage compartments, on the floors, every place there was a crack or crevice to fit a body. If a guy had a seat, it was no problem for a chick to sit on his lap. The twenty-five-hour trip was a madhouse of drinking tequila, singing, dancing, screwing in the seats, screwing on the floor, screwing in the large overhead luggage compartments, etc.

About halfway to Mazatlan, we pulled into a train station yard at midnight to switch locomotives and train crews. It would take about thirty minutes, so my roommate and I went looking for booze at a small station store and bought eight cheap pints of tequila. We sat down on a train platform and pulled out one of the pints from the brown bag and started drinking our newly procured nasty-tasting tequila and then frantically noticed our train was pulling out of the yard!

Son-of-a-bitch! We made a mad dash toward the train and had to dodge some train signals and stumble over train tracks in the dark but caught up near the locomotive engine and one of the Mexican engineers helped us up to the slow-moving locomotive. He had observed our comical run through the train yard and said we could join him and his partner in the locomotive's engineer compartment. His broken English explained it would be too dangerous to jump off and try to jump back onto the passenger cars behind the engine in our condition. My roommate and I wholeheartedly agreed realizing a panic-delayed tequila stupor was kicking in. We both sat on a bench in the back of the department and watch the two Mexicans move the train out of the yard and onto the main track.

What a childhood thrill to ride in the locomotive's engineer compartment, as we were later cruising along around forty miles an hour through the beautiful Mexican desert during a full moon. After about one hour, the two Mexican engineers pulled out brown packages and began eating their burrito meals. My roommate and I gave each Mexican a pint of tequila and watched them quickly drink it down like it was water. We gave another two pints to the very appreciative Mexicans but decided to keep the remaining two pints for us gringos.

Next, the Mexicans began singing and guitar playing with the drunk Mexicans moving to the back of the engine compartment and letting my roommate sit in the left front seat and I was allowed to sit in the right engineer's operating seat with my hand on the throttle lever. The Mexican engineer gave hand gestures to me about not moving the set throttle lever too much, which I eventually started slowly moving to a faster speed and then to a slower speed. I also began drunkenly blasting the train whistle as we passed a small village and I played simple song melodies on the whistle, too.

Suddenly, my roommate yelled and one of the Mexican engineers rushed over to me and pulled back the throttle lever. I hadn't comprehended the large Spanish "slow down for curve" sign and we began to careen to the left as we hit the oncoming curve going too fast.

After a seemingly prolonged panic, the train settled into a slower and less dangerous cruise along the tracks, and the engineer pointed to the back that I take a break from driving. I fully agreed and had the feeling to urgently vomit. I found the door to the outside and step out on a platform. My roommate followed me to keep me from falling off the train.

After puking downwind, I noticed a walkway with guard rails headed toward the front of the locomotive and convinced my roommate to take a stroll to the front of the engine. Eventually, we sat on the front cow catcher, which is a large iron device to "catch" cows that wander on the tracks and then get pushed and splattered away from the front of the locomotive engine.

It was such a beautiful night sitting on that cow catcher and observing the full moon hanging near the horizon. We had both forgotten about our wild speeding train curve experience, so it was just sitting back and gazing at the wondrous night sky.

Our tranquil train of thought was then brought to attention by the train whistle loudly blasting nonstop. We figured something was up and we both clambered back into the engineer's compartment.

As I entered the compartment first, one of the Mexicans was pointing ahead and shouting, "Mucho vaca, mucho vaca!"

My roommate hesitated in the doorway and I frowned at the word "vaca," and then my roommate poked his head back out to see what was ahead. Cows! Mucho vaca means mucho cows! The locomotive's large front light was now illuminating many cows that were wandering near the train tracks ahead. We hadn't noticed them earlier due to our serene tequila trance and quietly staring at the sky above

The Mexican abruptly pulled my roommate inside and slammed the door shut. Simultaneously, a loud thud shook the engine compartment as a large part of a cow's head and neck splattered onto the reinforced front window on the left side of the compartment. Blood and cow parts flew by where my roommate was previously standing in the open doorway.

Strangely, the engineer then sped up the train and hit another cow and the other engineer yelled in excitement and drank the remaining tequila from his last pint. The Mexican, who was not driving, then gave the engineer a few pesos.

My roommate looked at me and whispered, "They are taking bets on hitting the cows."

I whispered back, "I wonder what the bet would have been if we stayed there on the cow catcher?"

Another fifteen minutes passed by and the train stopped at a small station to pick up some cargo and mail. It was also time to join our friends in the back of the train. My roommate and I drunkenly said to the friendly engineers, "Adios and gracias," and we returned to a passenger car and found a place to pass out.

When we were in the passenger car and the train began pulling out of the small station, some of our friends shook us awake and asked where we were during the last few hours of the weird mayhem with the train ride.

For example, they asked us if we had heard strange and crazy train whistle sounds. They also asked if we felt the train shaking and leaning over and shuddering back to normal, and other people asked if we had seen parts of cows flying by and other oddities. My roommate and I just shrugged and said we were passed out for the past few hours. We both knew nobody would believe us anyway, except one guy bugged me about what I knew about a certain American singsong diddy he recognized and that no Mexican engineer would play it on the train whistle. I again shrugged and gave him a wry smile.

Mazatlan was terrific. I even met a beautiful 18-year-old senorita that I courted in the traditional Mexican way with two aunties following us wherever we went. It was love at first sight and I truly considered giving up school and settling in Mazatlan.

It was finally set up that I was to meet the whole family at the Catholic Church for the 10 o'clock morning mass. I had earlier mentioned that I was an altar boy and a good Catholic young man, so we would meet at church and I would join the family for later lunch and afternoon activities.

The problem was I had a hellacious night before, drinking tequila until six in the morning of the church date, and one of my friends dropped me off at the church at 9 o'clock to make sure I didn't miss my special meeting with the senorita's family. I didn't wear a watch in Mazatlan to try and sever my slavery from all time constraints on my life for once. But I didn't skip basic hygiene necessities and I did take a shower at the beach and wore fairly clean clothes. But I was horrifically hung over.

After trying not to pass out on the front of the church steps, I decided to enter the church during the 9 o'clock mass and stumbled into a church pew near the front and sat down to the glare of the Mexican priest who was in the middle of his sermon.

I sat there figuring I had this under control until two Mexican gentlemen were picking me off the floor under the pew at the directions of another priest, who had asked during his later sermon that I be taken out to sleep it off and snore outside.

I got outside and asked a kind-looking Mexican lady, "What time is it?"

She shook her head and then I pointed at her watch. She showed me her watch which read 11:40 am!

Later, my friend heard about my church fiasco and informed me that the senorita's family was not impressed with my church attendance and sat far away from me. He also told me the family owned quite a few businesses in Mazatlan and a beautiful big yacht that was anchored in the harbor.

Fucking tequila cost me big time.

After all the fun, screw-ups, and foolishness, I did graduate in 1970 with a very nice-looking Bachelor of Arts degree. I headed back to Los Angeles with extra confidence to succeed. Meanwhile, the U.S. Navy placed my enlistment on hold for various political reasons affecting the Vietnam War. Nonetheless, I was ready for my other war, i.e., the domestic war on affirmative action or any other obstacle to my future success.

1970-1978

Having a four-year university degree in my hand in the summer of 1970, I figured I could now get a good-paying job that was not adversely affected by the any zany affirmative action policies.

Initially, after applying for and being denied various good jobs because they had too many whites and, furthermore, I lacked the colorful qualifications needed for filling racial quotas, I did hear there was an immediate opening at my old gas station, which was not really the good-paying job I had in mind for a fairly decent white guy with a fancy university degree. But it was a job, and it would help me move out of my parents' spare bedroom and avoid being labeled the weird white guy who still lives with his parents.

When I contacted the gas station manager, he said that he needed someone who could immediately work the graveyard shift from midnight to morning. The shift was open because there was a rash of dangerous robberies occurring during the lonely early hours at gas stations in the whiter areas of L.A., and the manager's white graveyard guy had just quit out of fear for his life.

During this time of racial disharmony in L.A., a few white station attendants had been murdered by the group of black anti-whitey activists, who were robbing the stations and, according to police reports and racial epithets left at the scene, they were executing the white motherfuckers who were responsible for all their blackish problems.

What the hell, I said to myself, *desperate times to survive do create desperate reactionary measures.* I did own a gun and unbeknownst to the white gas station manager who embraced a pacifist point of view of a guilt-ridden white guy, I was becoming somewhat of a half-coward and half-crazed racial activist myself. Consequently, at the beginning of my first graveyard shift, I hung my diploma on the wall of the lubrication and oil change room and began work with my pistol hidden next to the floor safe for my personal protection. For what it's worth, the term "graveyard" shift took on a whole different meaning at the time of these racial confrontations.

After a rough two years working the night shift, which did have occasional below-freezing weather at my station and furthermore, having a few close calls with early morning drunks and some prickly people of color, a friend of mine came in the station and said there was an opening for a tech writer at the nearby Sperry Univac Company. He visited me in late December of 1972 when the nights were very cold, and he had recommended me for the job. I could definitely use a warmer and less hectic change of work environment and the very next day, I made an appointment for my interview in two days.

I got the job and gave my two weeks' notice and hoped I didn't get shot during my last days at the station. Overall, my time at the station did have some interesting moments, besides the unhinged drunk customers after the bars closed. Like the time I complained to the station manager that I felt guilty pumping gas in cars producing too much exhaust fumes, which added to the terrible smog conditions in the L.A. basin. He replied, "What's wrong with a brown sky?"

The Sperry job was a challenging but boring job, writing long complicated tech manuals, which probably explained why there were no affirmative action brothers demanding the position. On the bright side, the job was during the daylight hours and in an indoor temperature-controlled environment, due to the large and expensive computers that created software programs for U.S. military sub-chasing jets for the Navy.

Since all of Sperry's customers were military personnel that visited every few months to check on Sperry's progress and meeting certain program benchmarks, we, mostly white workers, gladly avoided meeting the general public and irate visitors of any color who could make white people's lives miserable when the oppressed colored people were in the mood.

After doing the tech writing job for eighteen months, I wanted a change since I was turning into a tech zombie.

On an impulse in mid-1974, I applied for a swimming pool cleaner in Beverly Hills, where racial turmoil seemed non-existent. I convinced the owner of the pool business to let me work for free for two weeks to prove myself capable and trustworthy while working at very expensive homes and among famous people. My pool cleaning trainer turned out to be a pleasant and hard-working Mexican, who taught me well and gave me a positive recommendation.

What a fantastic job that paid okay and it involved working around beautiful movie starlets lounging around incredible pools in skimpy bikinis that were gifts from the gods. It also took my mind off making the big bountiful bucks. Because now I was scoring major happy points while discreetly drooling over big bountiful boobs without getting caught and thrown in a jail cell full of perverts.

After cleaning pools for about a year and getting a few bucks ahead, I had a vacation break and took a trip to Tahiti. After ten "lost" days in Tahiti at a Club Med, where you basically walked around in a drunken stupor with alcohol credit beads hanging around your neck, I arrived back in L.A. and quit my pool cleaning job. I was still in a tropical stupor and didn't feel like working. I embraced a new lifestyle of "What the fuck, I'll do any random job just to get enough money for another island adventure."

I was enjoying being a cast away from important jobs that normal white guys coveted, and I didn't care what lucrative affirmative action jobs were being handed out to unqualified blacks. Furthermore, in mid-1975, I impetuously declared one day that I was going to be a writer and I sought out an exotic job to experience the underbelly of L.A. in order to gain the gritty experiences needed to augment my future Hemingway story-telling.

The adventurous under-belly job I landed was driving for Yellow Taxi Cab Company out of the most dangerous dispatch garage in L.A. It was the infamous Hollywood garage, which was right smack in the middle of L.A.'s finest wandering derelicts and dangerous loonies.

Around the Hollywood garage's vicinity and beyond, you had to navigate through countless criminals, drug addicts, prostitutes, weirdos, a challenging variety of sociopaths, gangs, and the bumbling gendarmes who tried to control the ever-present mayhem, i.e., the infamous L.A. County Sheriff's Department. Moreover, our drivers consisted of criminals on probation, drug addicts, weirdos, and sociopaths of all colors, including burned-out white guys trying to make a buck to keep them in booze and well-used broads. For some odd reason, a white guy with a college degree like me looking for adventure would occasionally appear for a driver's job, but most of these types of applicants fled the scene after meeting a few of the more disturbed maniacal cab drivers.

Somehow, I passed the interview with a gruff, fat, and always-angry supervisor, who I think wanted a token white jerk to experience a world totally outside my previous realm of pure white existence. He didn't realize that I survived racial combat experience during the Watts Riots, and I was ready for some new domestic violence, dwelling right inside America the Beautiful.

My Yellow Cab adventures lasted a year and I had witnessed so many under-belly activities I could write a book about L.A. taxi drivers. Nah, let's forget about that book. But one crazy chapter of near-violence to my cab and me I'll never forget.

It happened on an early summer morning around 1:30 am when I was negotiating my different fares to get close to the Los Angeles International Airport (LAX), which was the mecca for Yellow cabbies and big fares. But the problem for us Yellow cabbies getting into LAX, which had a sole service contract with Yellow Cab, was that you had to either bring a paying ride into the airport or begrudgingly accept a call to pick up a fare in treacherous south central L.A., which was the main center of L.A.'s criminal self-destruction and continuous black chaos.

The south-central pickup policy was a forced civil rights policy that Yellow Cab had adopted, after receiving multiple complaints from the black residents and the NAACP that cab drivers (even black drivers) would refuse to answer calls there, due to the high rate of robberies and cabbies being sent to the hospital for trying to collect their fares.

Knowing that the majority of people were taken to LAX by relatives or friends, Yellow Cab dispatchers would tempt us cabbies with "If you want to get into LAX, there's a ride available near Century Boulevard in south central, any takers?"

Most of the replies would be a combination of "Hell no!" and "Are you out of your fucking mind?!"

Eventually, a desperate cabbie needing some drug money or money to pay the rent on time like me would take a gamble and accept the call.

Previously heeding the advice of veteran drivers, which included the black drivers and my being new and not a fan of dangerous racial confrontations, I had always avoided south-central L.A. But I really needed to get into LAX for a big fare on that fateful early morning because I had recently received an apartment eviction warning.

So being real late on my rent payment, I accepted my first call into south central for a "Miss Shontella," a young lady needing a ride to visit her grandmother at the L.A. County Hospital.

She lived in a dangerous area near Century Boulevard and it was a straight shot on Century into central L.A. to the hospital. Besides, she needed to visit her mother at the hospital. What could go wrong?

As I approached and stopped at a rundown apartment on a dark street off Century, I felt a sudden chill on the warm L.A. early morning while waiting for my fare. I waited a few more minutes as some black drunks staggered by and peered into my partially open passenger window. I quickly felt the need for speed, as in getting the hell out of the place and screwing the LAX bonus.

However, a young black girl abruptly appeared at my open driver's window as I was looking out the other way, and she tapped me hard on the shoulder.

"Holy shit!" I gasped and nervously lurched around to see a twenty-something black girl stepping back and informing me she needed a quick cab ride. I hastily replied, "Okay, get in, I'm running late on my calls." Actually, the odds of my escaping south central intact were getting slimmer as each minute passed.

After she got into the backseat, she opened the other back door and a humongous black dude with a gigantic Afro hairdo jumped in and yelled, "Let's get the fuck outta here!"

I quickly pulled away from the curb and headed for Century Boulevard to drive east toward the hospital.

Something wasn't right, as the logic area of my anxious brain sounded a red alert. After driving a mile on Century, the black dude ordered me to pull over to the partially boarded-up liquor store with the iron grate front door. I stopped in front of the store and the black dude grumbled to his young lady friend, "I need you to get me some whiskey for the party." The lady friend seemed upset but obliged to Mr. King Kong and went into the liquor store.

"What party? What happened to the trip to the hospital? Oh, fuck," I said to myself. It was the old switcheroo trick that a wise black cabbie had previously warned me about. In order to get a cab to come into the south-central jungle, the blacks would make up a pleasant-sounding reason to be picked up; for example, I need to visit my synagogue, or I need to visit a sick relative in the hospital, etc. Then once they were picked up, it was to take them to their Black Panther meeting or drive them to the nearest riot against the fucking whitey oppressors. AAAAHHHHH!

The location where I parked near the liquor store was in an area right out of a horror film called, "Guess What Dumb Ass White Cab Drive Invaded Our Hood to Get Fucked Up and Robbed!"

Of course, it didn't take long for the black dude to brandish his weapon and grumbled he wanted all my money.

Due to a slow night, I only had twenty-two dollars and change, which upset my black friend pointing a gun at my head. He waved at a few of his "cousins" who were standing outside the liquor store to come over to the cab. He complained to them about the small shit-ass amount of "donated" money he had taken from this chalk dick driver. All his cousins started grumbling about what they gonna do to this disrespectful white motherfucker. The big black dude got out of the cab and said, "Let's show this whitey ass what we think about him and his whitey company."

They all commenced to start pissing on and in my cab through the open cab windows in the front and back seats—my cab had a busted air conditioner, and I kept the windows open for ventilation. The big black dude then yelled at me, "What the fuck you all gonna do about it?"

After pausing a minute to try to fully comprehend my urinated-on predicament, I got out of my cab, joined them, and started pissing on the cab, too.

In a moment of changed animosity toward me and my cab, the brothers started laughing and pointing at me. They were either laughing at me or my short white dick or both. I didn't care. There was now communal conviviality and camaraderie amongst the pungent smell of urine emanating from my cab and my pants after I also pissed down my leg in all the excitement.

In the meantime, the young black girl came out the liquor store door and shook her head, saying, "What you fools doing?" She then told her big black boyfriend that she called her sister and that she was coming over to pick them up because the party location got changed and she didn't know the place.

Everything began to calm down and the young black girl surprised me and slipped me a five-dollar bill without King Kong knowing it and told me to get the hell out of south central.

I completely agreed and tried to thank her for the tip, but she quickly said, "Shaddup and leave, fool."

It didn't take long for me to be speeding toward the airport. I called dispatch and said I finished my south-central pickup and would be entering LAX shortly. He said I had to prove it, and I said I could when I finished my shift and he inspected my cab.

After arriving at my busy LAX taxi stand, I was soon approached by a newly arrived and tired traveler who needed to go a long way from the airport. This was great news since I had just donated all my money, except for five bucks, to the Black Poverty and Thug Foundation of South Central L.A.

The male fare had no luggage and he climbed into the back seat. Regrettably, after quickly driving out of the airport, my fare was squirming in the backseat and wanting me to drop him off at the nearest hotel. I guess his jet lag and my PTSD from the south-central pissing incident had numbed our sense of smell, and we both finally realized that there was a really bad stench in my cab.

I complied with his wishes and dropped him off at the first hotel I saw. He paid the small fare and remarked that my cab's backseat was wet and smelled atrocious like someone had pissed on it. I told him I had a long night and just had a bad experience in a rough part of town. He appeared sympathetic, even though he cringed at the feel of the damp backside of his pants, and he did give me a fairly nice tip for my troubles. If he only knew the troubles I've been going through to gain some Hemingway experience.

Since I couldn't go back into LAX without violating company policy and my shift was nearly over, I headed back to the Hollywood garage and parked on the roof parking area.

The maintenance cleaning crew gave a quick inspection of my cab and started cleaning the exterior but stopped when they got a good whiff of the interior.

One cleaner then called the supervisor on his radio and reported the very pungent problem. I had to meet with my early morning supervisor and explained the terrible urine stench in my cab. He wasn't very happy with the smelly situation but gave me a break when he realized that I had a dangerous encounter in south-central L.A., although he gruffly reminded me that the company felt its cabs were worth much more than us measly drivers who could be easily replaced.

On my way out of the supervisor's office which was close to the company's cab washing facility, I noticed through the open sides of the washing facility that my cab was being mechanically pulled through the cab washer with its doors wide open.

That same day in the early evening when I reported back for my late night shift, I noticed my previously pissed-on cab was now parked in a corner having its interior still drying out with the doors still wide open. To add insult to injury, I had my next paycheck deducted for a gallon of industrial-strength deodorizer.

Like I said earlier, I lasted a year at Yellow Cab and the under-belly madness of most of L.A. Furthermore, I had enough food and partial rent money to take a short and much-needed break.

My meager savings didn't last too long, and I luckily stumbled upon a unique and fair-paying job in the early summer of 1976 at ABC Messenger Service, which was located in a nicer part of Hollywood and serviced the expansive L.A. movie industry.

ABC Messenger appeared to have a monopoly on all the important documents and miscellaneous deliveries to the movie studios, movie producers, and movie stars and agents in Hollywood. As a fledgling and naïve writer, what better way to present a movie screenplay to a movie executive or movie star while you were delivering special documents to them? As it turned out, it was such a good job meeting famous people that I didn't want to spoil it by trying to naively pitch my rookie writing to busy and accomplished movie professionals.

Besides, there were unwritten rules when making your ABC deliveries, and any unwanted displays of nosiness, unnecessary talking, or trying to make moves for your own self-interests were strongly forbidden. If you violated these rules, you would lose your job if it was reported to the ABC business manager. It was tempting and some opportunities were there for the taking, but I resisted the temptations and just enjoyed the fascinating job.

But I have to confess, that while avoiding bothering the movie execs and other important movie people, I did get a great opportunity with a famous movie producer named Mr. Walter Mirisch.

After working several months at ABC, I was placed in the top three delivery guys for on-time deliveries, prudent actions when making professional deliveries, and not bugging the stars or selling "behind the scenes" stories to sleazy tabloids and magazines.

It happened on one of my favorite but rare deliveries to the top of the Universal Tower Building, where powerful Mr. Mirisch had this absolutely magnificent and overwhelming office with an exceptionally wise and efficient front office assistant.

His assistant, who was a no-nonsense tigress, protected Mr. Mirisch from any unwanted bullshit or any unwanted screenplays or "special" projects, which I and other delivery guys would deliver to his office.

My deliveries were always screenplays that were delivered at an extra cost and the special deliveries were either paid for by an anxious agent or writer. The extra cost included my immediately calling the agent or writer right after the delivery and telling them that I had personally hand-delivered the screenplay right into Mr. Mirisch's hands. I would then have to describe what Mr. Mirisch's honest reaction was to the delivered item.

Most secretaries or assistants for powerful producers would routinely call their bosses and then sign for the delivery without the producer getting involved.

But I was lucky. Mr. Mirisch was a gracious man and he knew I had to normally fulfill a special request for a delivery personally to him. Subsequently, he would advise his assistant to allow me to come into his office and we would have a short chat while he signed my delivery slip. He would then instruct me to hand the screenplay to his assistant, who was an excellent judge of material.

After giving his assistant the screenplay, she would scan the writer's name and the first three pages of the screenplay and inevitably toss it in the trash can every time I made a delivery. Maybe some other deliveries made it past her quick and straightforward judgment, but not any of mine.

After witnessing the real world of what really happened to the screenplays I delivered to Mr. Mirisch's office, I had to be very diplomatic and make the special call to a very anxious agent or writer. I was allowed to call the agent or writer from the assistant's office of Mr. Mirisch and proceeded to give a nice bullshit story that the screenplay was delivered, it was given special "consideration," and it was being kept in a special (circular) file. I figured my own novice screenplay if it ever reached Mr. Mirisch's office, would be set on fire in the trash can.

On one occasion during my mercy call to a nervous writer, Mr. Mirisch's assistant seemed amused by my forced "diplomacy" concerning the trashed screenplay, and she also enjoyed bugging me about where I was hiding my own screenplay treatment. Was it in my back pocket or jacket? I would tell her that I stayed away from that trick to get my work submitted and also, I wasn't quite ready yet with my first writing project.

On that occasion, Mr. Mirisch came out of his office and joined the conversation with the assistant about my not having the confidence to getting my project finished. Mr. Mirisch told me to just be confident and finish a treatment for review.

Having been fortunate to enjoy a great relationship with Mr. Mirisch and his assistant, the assistant, with Mr. Mirisch's nod of approval, said she would give my treatment a read-through and even help me develop it within the studio system if it had any potential.

Wow, what an opportunity, and Mr. Mirisch seemed so sincere with the offer that I felt super blessed about the break.

Time went by and I got another delivery to Mr. Mirisch's office. After the delivery, the assistant asked to see my screenplay treatment. I stammered and said it wasn't completed yet. She just shook her head and she appeared to change her supportive attitude toward me. She then sternly said, "You know in this business, you jump at any opportunity immediately, and you just blew it."

This hit me like a ton of bricks, and I knew I had blown a huge writing opportunity and a chance to get my big goofy foot in the movie industry's door. From my overall experience dealing with movie people, when you're asked to perform, you perform without hesitation, not later. I sensed I left Mr. Mirisch's office probably for the last time.

Later, I felt really down about my insecure shortcomings in something I sincerely liked to do, which could have provided me with paid escapism from my personal battle with self-doubt and ongoing social upheaval. Some of life's lessons are hard to swallow.

After New Year's Day in 1977, I began thinking about my options and I decided after a year I would leave the U.S. mainland and find a tropical island in which to get lost as I did in Tahiti. Maybe the solitude of island living would encourage me to write and re-write and then re-write, if necessary, in order to complete a writing project for possible submittal.

I knew that practicing long physical hours in sports enabled me to achieve my goals in my earlier sports career. But I also realized that professional writing is not only the physical part of moving the pen or typing on a keyboard. It also involves practicing mental exercises to conquer one's self-doubt to overcome the fear of making mistakes, and the problems of procrastination to avoid the possibility of personal failures. I needed to be able to satisfactorily finish a written project, which would be good for my soul, and for whatever reason that my personal accomplishment would serve in the scheme of life.

It was almost the spring of 1977, and I was still working at ABC Messenger. One night, I had an important delivery to make in the lobby of the Motion Picture Academy Awards Show before it was going to be aired live on national television. It was a delivery for Mr. Mirisch, who was then the President of the Academy of Motion Picture Arts and Sciences. I felt embarrassed to approach Mr. Mirisch after my writing failure at his office and wanted a production assistant to make the delivery to him. But Mr. Mirisch saw me and called out, "Hey, Jack, come on over here."

I went over to him, and it was heartening that he had remembered my name. He accepted the delivery as he introduced me as a friend to the three people he was talking with at the time. They were Kirk Douglas, Burt Lancaster, and Robert Mitchum.

For a Hollywood dreamer, to have met and gotten to know a gracious Hollywood legend like Mr. Mirisch was a gift from the movie-making gods. His pleasant demeanor and the sincere friendliness that he extended to me were a boost to my floundering ego.

Even though he was in a discussion with three of the biggest stars in Hollywood, he made time to ask me if I had delivered my treatment to his assistant, and I stammered, "Sorry, Mr. Mirisch, I blew it and plan leaving for a small Pacific Island to get my writing act together."

He was somewhat bewildered by my blunt admission of failure and a desire to flee to some island, as if "wouldn't it be better to enroll in a screenplay writing class somewhere in L.A.?"

He signed my delivery receipt and wished me good luck. I sincerely replied, "Thanks for everything."

I then nodded to Mr. Douglas, Mr. Lancaster, and Mr. Mitchum, and they slightly nodded back and continued talking with Mr. Mirisch.

I finally resigned from ABC Messenger in early December of 1977, in order to begin my island quest for personal salvation.

On the morning of New Year's Day of 1978, and after a heavy night of New Year's celebrating and drinking, I passed out on my good friends' couch and ended up staying with them due to my meager funds and the loss of my apartment at the end of December.

In the first part of March, I found the island where I wanted to hide out. It happened when my friend and I were drinking beer and tequila shots in his backyard, and we were talking nonsense as he was reading the L.A. Times. He started reading parts of a story out loud about a new U.S. Commonwealth of the Northern Mariana Islands, which had been recently created in Micronesia in the Western Pacific Ocean. The story stated that the new commonwealth would receive a ton of federal aid and benefits with its joining the U.S. family, and it sparked my interest.

He continued reading and saying that the commonwealth islands had about 8000 islander inhabitants, who mostly lived on the main island of Saipan. Then unbeknownst to me, my friend drunkenly misread that Saipan had only one bar owned by an ex-U.S. Navy white guy named Chief Wilburn Hamilton.

As we pondered this situation in a drunken stupor, this friend of mine mentioned he had access to a liquor distributor and he slurred that this was the ideal island for me to set up camp, open bar number two, and write whenever the urge presented itself.

He kept joking that he would supply me with cheap booze, and I finally said, "Why not?" We then proceeded to both pass out in his patio lounge chairs.

The next day when I was sober enough, I drove to the nearest library and read that the island of Saipan was located 120 miles north of the U.S. territory of Guam and approximately 1500 miles southeast of Japan. From the few pictures in the library's information book and some pictures of young and pretty island girls that I had earlier seen in the L.A. Times article, it appeared to be a really nice place with a pleasant tropical climate and friendly island females. The problem was my serious lack of travel and island survival funds since I quit my ABC job in early December.

I only had a few bucks and owned a used Subaru worth maybe 600 bucks. When I called Continental Airlines, which flew to Micronesia, I was told the fare to Saipan would be 720 dollars. I asked about cheaper fares and the customer rep said they had a missionary fare for just under 400 dollars. Missionary fare? I hung up the phone and concocted my airline travel scheme.

I waited about fifteen minutes to avoid talking to the same rep and called Continental Airlines again.

After inquiring about fares to Saipan, I was informed by a different rep that Continental Airlines traveled to Hawaii, and then its partner, Continental Air Micronesia, connected to Saipan in Micronesia for a total fare of 720 dollars.

I replied with my fake story that I was a missionary and inquired if there was a missionary fare to Saipan. The rep stated that there was a one-way missionary fare for 375, but I had to answer a few questions first; for example: Which religious group or order was I a member of? Answer: "Brothers of Saint Alemany." Which mission or church would I visit? Answer: Mount Carmel Catholic Church and School on Saipan (that I had earlier learned about in the library).

After passing my missionary quiz and booking my reservation, I immediately went to a combination used car lot and pawn shop and sold my car for 475 dollars. I later went to the San Fernando Mission and bought a small wooden cross to wear around my neck. I then proceeded to a barber shop for a short missionary haircut to replace my hippie long hair that hung down to my shoulders.

The next day, I called another friend of mine who was a regular writer for a popular television sitcom, and she agreed to take me to the airport the following morning. Things were really happening fast.

I quickly threw my stuff in an old Navy bag, which had belonged to my dad, and then I celebrated my departure from civilization that night with my friend and his wife at their house where I was staying.

The following morning, I was driven to the airport by my writer friend, who was also a friendly critic of my own botched writing career.

As we traveled to LAX airport, I sat in her car proudly wearing my "missionary travel attire," i.e., dark slacks and a nice white shirt with a small wooden cross around my neck.

My friend just shook her head at my outfit and new missionary haircut and said that if I failed with this new adventure, I should call her and she would send me money to head back to civilization.

When we pulled up to the departure area at LAX, she curiously asked me about my unfinished sci-fi screenplay treatment, which I had earlier confessed to her that I had messed up with Mr. Mirisch. She finally inquired again, "Well, are you going to finish it?"

I replied that I was still on page three, waved goodbye, and disappeared into the crowd at L.A. International Airport.

While waiting in line to check in, I made a promise to myself that I would finish the screenplay on Saipan, in honor of Mr. Mirisch and the support he extended to me when we interacted. I knew I would never forget his kindness and his desire to see me accomplish some sort of success with my writing.

1978-1992

I arrived on Saipan Island at the prime age of 31 on March 17, 1978—St. Patrick's Day—with one faded Navy bag, one pair of pants, two shirts, one wooden cross, one pair of black low-cut Converse basketball shoes, some underwear and swimming trunks, my carpenter's belt & bags with my hammer and tools, my college diploma stuck inside with the tools for extra support to get any kind of job available, and other odds and ends. I also had my initial island survival savings of 92 bucks tucked safely in my front pocket.

After leaving the departure area, I ended up sitting on an old bench by the airport roadside in the early evening and asked myself, "Now, what the hell do I do?"

Thirty minutes later, the entire airport area was completely empty at the relatively small airport, except for a large island security guard dressed in a loose-fitting tattered uniform and wearing flip-flops.

Some more time elapsed and an old truck stopped near where I was anxiously sitting. An elderly islander was driving with his grandson in the front seat. He asked if I needed a ride and I said, "Sure."

Since there was no room in the front seat, I had to jump into the rear of the truck bed and joined a dog tied to a large cement block near the front of the truck bed. I also joined some chickens that had their legs tied to an old wooden crate. The dog seemed safe enough, as long as I sat at the back of the truck bed, and I did feel grateful for my first taste of island hospitality with the free ride. But I also had mixed feelings about sitting near a suspicious growling dog and some agitated chickens who were flapping their wings and blowing dried chicken poop debris in my face.

The old man drove me to his wooden house and dropped off his grandson. Then without inviting me into the front seat, he drove me into the main village that had the one small and aging beachside hotel in the "downtown" part of the island.

He dropped me off at the hotel and as I was sneezing and climbing out of the back of his truck, he told me this was the hotel where an occasional white U.S. statesider would stay until he relocated to free housing after reporting for work at the U.S. Trust Territory of the Pacific Islands (TTPI) government headquarters on Capitol Hill.

As I was scoping out the rundown hotel and the cheap room rates, a friendly young islander guy in his mid-twenties approached me in the lobby and asked me, an obvious newcomer to the island, to join him for some island sightseeing.

Feeling the need to get acquainted with my new home with a friendly inhabitant, I left my Navy luggage bag at the front desk, and we both left the lobby and jumped into his old car. We went straight to a nearby bar to drink some cheap booze and sightsee the imported young Filipina bar girls.

Apparently, drinking and buying inexpensive ladies' drinks for the young bar girls, who would then sit on your lap for a spell, were the favorite pastimes on this isolated rock in the middle of nowhere.

Eventually, I found out that there were several Saipan bars that were nicely stocked with imported young waitresses from the Philippines on this thirsty and entertainment-starved island. Furthermore, thinking back to the time I got very inebriated drinking tequila with my friend on his patio, I realized that he had drunkenly misread the part about there being only one bar on Saipan.

At last, I got back to the hotel after midnight with only two dollars in my pocket and no money for even a cheap hotel room and had to sleep on the beach during my first night on lovely Saipan Island.

In the early morning, a friendly front desk clerk found me passed out on the beach. He nudged me awake and told me that the islander who took me out drinking was his cousin. And since his cousin was mostly responsible for blowing my meager life savings for drinks for all his "cousins," the island custom was for the hotel clerk to return my generosity to his cousins and give me a free room for a few days until I got my free TTPI government housing.

After contemplating my predicament, I didn't reveal to the hotel clerk that I had no job at the TTPI government and had only two bucks. So, I accepted his kind offer of getting my second taste of island hospitality—without having to inhale dried chicken poop up my nose.

Five days later, it was discovered by the hotel management that I had no job at the TTPI and I freely admitted it. I was warned that several of the islanders were anti-American toward statesiders for one reason or another, and I needed to be careful to not disrespect the brown islanders or it could lead to big trouble for my white stateside butt.

It was lucky for me that the hotel manager was sympathetic to my situation and allowed me to stay a few more days. He was an elderly islander who practiced the ancient island culture of providing goodwill to needy outsiders, but I was also wary of island customs like a naive outsider paying for all the drinks for several island "cousins." I told the manager that I was seeking a job teaching at Mount Carmel Catholic School, and that I would pay my bill for the room and the food I charged as soon as possible.

As it turned out, I was hired to teach elementary students for 15-20 hours a week at 60 cents an hour, which would take me a long time to pay my hotel bill of 120 bucks.

Fortunately, the hotel manager discounted my bill and even allowed me to stay at the hotel a little while longer since I was teaching at the local island school. I guess he sort of liked me because I was one of the few white statesiders on the island without a nice TTPI government job and who had decided to work and live among the islanders in one of the local villages on Saipan.

Most of the 8,000 indigenous islanders (mainly Chamorros and Carolinians) lived on Saipan at the time, with nearly a thousand living on each of the outer islands of Rota and Tinian. On Saipan, there were a few statesiders living in various local villages, although there were approximately 100 white statesiders working and living on secluded Capitol Hill, which was the headquarters of the U.S. Trust Territory of the Pacific Islands. The TTPI consisted of the Micronesian islands of Palau, Marshall Islands, Truk, Ponape, Kosrae, and Yap. All these islands the U.S. military had occupied and had claimed possession from Japan after World War II.

Saipan, which is approximately six miles wide and 16 miles long, is one of the three inhabited islands that comprised the U.S. Commonwealth of the Northern Mariana Islands (CNMI). The CNMI was a part of the TTPI prior to 1978, but in late 1977, it finally voted to be a separate U.S. commonwealth by a "yes" vote of approximately 70 percent.

I had chosen to live in the main village of Chalan Kanoa below Capitol Hill, and I was the only white guy living among the islanders in the main village. To put it in historical racial perspective, I was officially a MINORITY person, who should, according to the U.S. Civil Rights Act of 1964, be accorded all the rights and privileges of being a person of color. Although being absent of any "color," it was open for debate if I actually qualified for any type of ethnic protection.

Moreover, with approximately 30 percent of the indigenous islanders voting against becoming a U.S. commonwealth and opposing any U.S. "statesider" Civil Rights laws, among other stupid U.S. laws, the thirty percenters frankly told me to kiss their brown butts. I have to admit it was quite dangerous at times living in the main village, and the whites at the TTPI government advised me to get a job at the TTPI pronto and live in relative safety on Capitol Hill.

Naturally, the crazy streak that kept lingering within my rebellious brain made me stick it out and challenge the island gods. Plus, I wanted to shed the nagging feeling of being a white coward.

My growing acceptance by the local islanders, who were mostly Catholic and included many of the maniacal 30 percenters, was greatly assisted by my being a fairly well-liked and decent teacher at the local Catholic elementary school.

The school principal was an islander and former nun who had frankly told me I was an emergency hire and that she didn't trust white people.

I honestly told her that after being jumped and involved in several fist fights with the island's church-going and anti-American 30 percenters, I really didn't trust brown people either.

During our previously frank racial exchange, the principal shook her head at my not trusting brown people and just stared at me, probably thinking "Doesn't this clueless white statesider know that he is outnumbered by a bunch of anti-American brown islanders and he's trapped on a small island?"

I stared back at her and smiled, and she for the first time smiled at me. I think we eventually called it a draw and became "guarded" friends during my teaching days at Mount Carmel as the only white teacher at the school.

The principal even rented a bedroom to me after I had left the hotel and had been living on the beach. The 10-dollar-a-month room was in her old, abandoned family home that had no water, electricity, windows, or doors. There was another low-income renter living there who was a Filipino laborer and stayed in the bigger living room for 15 dollars a month. We eventually got electricity from a long extension cord from a nice islander neighbor on one side of the house, and our water was supplied by a hose with a shut-off valve that hung over the fence on the other side of the house from another kindly local neighbor. Yes, we showered naked outside just prior to the morning daylight before going to work. Home sweet home in paradise.

Overall, I sensed I was on my way to partially shedding my self-doubt and white cowardice, and even began thinking about writing a great screenplay. Then I would return to Mr. Mirisch's office and eventually receive my future Oscar. Oh yeah, now I was truly living in Saipan Tropical Dreaming.

Two months later in June of 1978, I was suddenly recruited to run the main amusement attraction on Saipan, i.e., the Saipan Bowling Center. It was previously managed by a local islander who didn't keep it running too well. Of course, his being relieved of command and being replaced by the only white guy in the village was not very well received by several of the more dangerous island's thirty percenters.

In spite of several threats against my bodily safety, I did work hard to clean and rebuild the dilapidated facility inside and out, and the locals did appreciate my efforts to provide them with a nice place to hang out. I fixed all the bowling lanes, thoroughly cleaned the snack bar, and provided healthy food without cockroaches running around their plates. I also fixed up the restrooms for proper use, fixed the air conditioner to nicely cool everyone's brown butts, remodeled an area for a bar and dance lounge, hired a good band, and, finally, due to several threats, I bought a .38 caliber revolver from a congenial island cop who recommended that I carry a concealed weapon to protect my white butt.

The friendly cop had advised me that there seem to be rumors floating around that some of the 30 percenters were talking about having an island-style massacre of one very white U.S. statesider, who took the manager's job away from a local islander at the bowling center. Ironically, having a handgun was against the local law, except if you were a cop or a local bad guy on the island. But I had wisely supplied enough free beer to many of the local police officers in exchange for certain favors and one very nice pistol and even some illegal bullets, which caused another rumor that the crazy statesider would shoot back.

All in all, it was a wild and wacky time at the bowling center, and I even married a young Palauan island girl who liked to bowl. She was even tougher than some of the island punks, who wanted to throw me into an active volcano, and she was very pretty too!

After about 18 months of island shenanigans at the bowling center and elsewhere, I left Saipan to return to the U.S. mainland for a short civilization refresher for my frazzled mental outlook on life.

In February of 1980, I returned to Saipan and rejoined my island wife, who also needed a break from a semi-wild statesider. I eventually got a job working at the TTPI government HQ as an energy consultant. The TTPI hiring office noticed that I had pumped gas during my U.S. college days in the early 1970s and, bingo, I qualified as an island expert in energy matters.

My main job was to inventory the multitude of air conditioners in the large TTPI complex and to not criticize the bumbling white stateside male TTPI managers for having too many energy-wasting air cons in their super refrigerated headquarters. Nearly all the obese stateside TTPI managers hated to sit and sweat as they read magazines and counted their bonus pay for toiling in the tropical jungle.

Moreover, since the U.S. currently had a Democratic president who appointed all the bumbling liberal Democrats for the well-paying positions at the TTPI, I was soon advised by a few trusted TTPI co-workers to be quiet about my personal politics and don't mention my preferred candidate for the upcoming U.S. presidential election in November of 1980. My candidate was a product from my good old days working in Hollywood. He was the actor and former California governor, Ronald Reagan.

Reagan was a staunch conservative Republican and was really hated by the liberal Democratic higher-ups at the TTPI headquarters.

On a spur of the moment, I mailed a five-dollar donation to the Reagan campaign office in Washington, D.C., and two months later—and just two weeks before the election—I received a large manila envelope from D.C., which raised a few liberalized eyebrows in the TTPI mailroom. This envelope included two campaign posters, a "signed" print of an artist's portrait of a rugged-looking and smiling Reagan wearing a cowboy hat, and my own official plastic membership card for the U.S. Republican National Committee.

My energy co-worker advised me to hide the Reagan paraphernalia. But that rebellious crazy streak always lurking in my brain urged me to tape my Reagan campaign posters on the wall in my work cubicle, which were promptly torn down by the night cleaning crew by orders of the TTPI pissed-off management.

In somewhat of a surprise win, the actor Reagan soundly beat the Democrat Jimmy Carter. Naturally, the TTPI "powers that be" freaked out. As a result, I became a victim of a frenzied retaliatory move and I was abruptly terminated for some trumped-up charges, e.g., theft of cheap government pens, being a Republican pervert, and being always drunk on the job (which was only partly true). In a show of typical Democratic graciousness in accepting a resounding defeat of their liberal and looney policies, I was stripped of my TTPI badge and my cubicle nameplate was ripped off the wall and tossed into the trashcan, and then I was ceremoniously escorted out of the building by the whole TTPI security team.

After my abrupt banishment from Capitol Hill, I returned to my humble Saipan beginnings in the quaint village of Chalan Kanoa and pondered my latest Saipan predicament.

However, the island gods do exhibit charmed karma toward certain talented but strange statesiders in the quirky island scheme of things.

Being out of work for several months—but luckily having a hard-working Palauan wife to support me and having some remaining TTPI severance pay—I had plenty of free time to think about my next move, and all indications were pointing to my being somehow rescued from my island poverty and my semi-joblessness. I did earn a few bucks as a Saipan news stringer for the Pacific Daily News (PDN), which was a Micronesian newspaper outlet on the bigger island of Guam.

One night while thinking and drinking in my favorite bar on Saipan called Hamilton's, which was owned by retired U.S. Navy CPO Wilburn Hamilton who had married a beautiful local island girl, I concocted a scheme for a new job with the help of Chief's crafty wisdom.

Chief Hamilton was one of the few other white guys living in the local villages below Capitol Hill, along with some newly arrived, burned-out white stateside attorneys who assisted the local government's island leaders in writing grants and proposals for lucrative federal handouts.

Chief, as Hamilton was always called, had asked me while I was thinking less and drinking much more why in the hell I came to Saipan without any money or unique island skills to keep a steady job.

I told Chief about a drunken friend of mine in Southern California who told me there was only one bar on Saipan and we could be partners in a successful second bar, which was a drunk distortion of reality that was concocted by the inebriated misreading of an L.A. Times news article about Saipan.

So, I blamed my California friend and the Chief for my island trials and tribulations. Chief just laughed and then showed me the L.A. Times news article, which was sent to him by the L.A. Times reporter who was on Saipan to cover the first commonwealth gubernatorial inauguration in January of 1978.

The article quoted Chief who said he had the only "stateside" bar on Saipan and it mainly catered to the white statesiders on the island, including the TTPI white mob, and some local islanders related to his popular island wife.

I admitted to Chief that too much tequila can do strange things to a person's ability to get the facts straight. Although I just knew there had to be more than one bar on little Saipan Island where there was not much to do but drink and chase island girls.

Frankly slurring, I told Chief that after seeing the beautiful island girls in the L.A. Times and learning about the fairly pleasant tropical island atmosphere (besides the infamous 30 percenters), I wanted to come to Saipan to accomplish my Hemingway goal to achieve a prosperous writing career and enjoy entering a special writer's Valhalla. Chief gave me a quizzical look and pour himself another large dose of Canadian Club.

Chief was known to be a knowledgeable Saipan bartender/advisor, and he eventually said to me that since the local commonwealth government was having its own gubernatorial election soon in November of 1981, and if the local Saipan Republican candidate got elected as Reagan did, I could probably get a job because I was an official card-carrying member of the U.S Republican National Committee and a bona fide supporter and possible personal confidant of President Ronald Reagan himself.

As a result of Chief's advice and his wise and canny recommendation to strategically stretch the truth when dealing with the somewhat naïve local islanders, I took the last of my remaining TTPI severance pay and bought a not-too-expensive full-page campaign ad in the local newspaper. It was in support of the Republican candidate for the upcoming CNMI governor's election and I even had an enlarged copy of my official Republican National Committee membership card printed at the bottom of the ad.

Hallelujah! The local Republican Party thought I was some kind of big-shot Reagan supporter—and all for only a five-buck donation that nobody knew about except maybe some dimwitted Democratic TTPI managers who were terminated and left Saipan earlier. I was immediately invited to join the local campaign and dispense with Republican wisdom all over the place.

The local Republican gubernatorial candidate did win and I was later appointed the governor's Public Information Officer (PIO) in February of 1982. I was judged "qualified" to be the media representative and advisor to the governor, which was based on my short stint as a Saipan news stringer for the Pacific Daily News and my supportive news articles about the new Republican governor. Furthermore, my being labeled a media expert on Saipan didn't take very much actual experience as long as I could speak English fairly coherently and could write big sentences.

The years that followed were a blur of travel around the world and working for a great island leader, Governor Pedro P. Tenorio, who appreciated my loyalty, hard work, and even my occasional trips into innocent tropical lunacy. For instance…

Dear Pete and Sophie

It was in early March of 1982, and I accompanied the Governor to Washington, D.C. for the Annual Governors' Meeting and a meet and greet dinner with President Ronald Reagan.

While waiting at the front of the Hyatt Regency Hotel for a limousine to pull up and take the Governor, his First Lady Sophie, and me to a special White House Dinner, I saw the former Miss America, Phyllis George, the wife and First Lady of the Governor of

Kentucky, John Y. Brown Jr., and she was sitting in a nearby limo. I was awe-struck by her beauty, and for some impulsive reason, I climbed into her limo like I was one of her aides. I sat across from her and the Kentucky Governor and was situated between two legitimate aides in a row of seats facing her. After about an awkward minute or two passed as the limo was slowly leaving, the Kentucky First Lady squinted at me and then in a fit of exasperation asked me, "Who in the hell are you?"

I quickly explained to her, "When I was waiting for my Governor's limo, I was standing near the Kentucky limo and I was told by a security guard, who thought I was a Kentucky aide, to hurry up and get in your limo because the traffic was backing up and I just thought I could get a ride with you and your nice husband to the president's dinner." The bemused Kentucky Governor slightly laughed and asked if I really wanted to just meet his wife because I was a fan of hers. I said, "Of course, especially because of her days as a TV sports reporter."

First Lady Phyllis didn't see the humor in my being in the limo, and I was instructed to exit immediately, or she would notify security. The Kentucky limo then came to a sudden stop and I maneuvered around the aide nearest to the door and exited. Due to my long and confusing explanation of what happened with the Kentucky limo to the hotel's security supervisor, I missed my ride with my own Governor to the White House where I could have hung out with President Reagan and even some fellow governors' aides and swap stories, like my unauthorized meeting with gorgeous Phyllis George.

The next day, my Governor asked what happened to me about my missing the White House affair. I told him it was a long story and he just smiled, knowing my penchant to get side-tracked and going AWOL at times.

Later the same day I bought an official postcard of a White House portrait of President Reagan and First Lady Nancy Reagan. I wrote on it a special presidential message to Governor Tenorio and his lovely wife, saying, "Dear Pete and Sophie, Nancy and I had a great time dancing the boogie-woogie and singing with you at the White House party. Let's do it again!" I signed it "Ron & Nancy" and mailed it to my Governor's San Diego address in California, where he kept a stateside house for a few older relatives, who were the guardians for his younger children who were attending school in San Diego.

Two weeks later when the Governor and I were both back on Saipan Island, the Governor asked me if I knew anything about a strange postcard that was mailed to his San Diego house from Washington, D.C.

I inquired about what kind of postcard. The Governor said it was a postcard supposedly mailed by President Reagan to his house in San Diego and his youngest child took it to school for a show-and-tell activity. The Governor then told me a nice story about his youngest child who proudly read the card to her third grade class. However, the teacher was suspicious about the frivolity of the message and checked the Governor's older child about the authenticity of the card. Then the Governor's older daughter called her mother, the First Lady, who checked the Governor concerning a weird story about a boogie-woogie party with "Ron and Nancy." They both realized that in all likelihood it had to be a prank card sent by someone a bit goofy and who was the only traveling aide with the Governor to Washington for the Annual Governors' Meeting. Besides, the Governor and First Lady only met with President Reagan and his First Lady in person during a short photo op.

The Governor waited for my next response and after being trapped like a cornered but loyal rat, I admitted that I was the Governor's only traveling aide who accompanied him to D.C.

I then waited for the Governor to react. He stared at me for a moment shaking his finger and then laughed. Like I said, he was a great Governor and a great guy, and he treated me as a friend. But as I got up to leave his office, he did advise me to not do that again, or his wife might have me fired for pranking her husband and her, who also happened to be the Honorable CNMI Governor and First Lady.

Moreover, the Governor also asked me to find out through my media connections who was the dumb idiot who had painted a big green shamrock on our airport's runway, which was being investigated by a Federal Aviation Agency (FAA) official based on Guam Island. I gulped and said "Sure, I'll do my best."

The Green Shamrock Runway

The truth of the matter was that I was drinking in Chief Hamilton's a few days earlier and we were celebrating Saint Patrick's Day. I had exceeded the official coherency zone by downing seven or maybe was it ten shots of tequila, and Hamilton, who said he had some Irish blood in him mixed with an excessive amount of Canadian Club that night, shouted out that someone had do something spectacular for good ol' Saint Paddy.

Well, to make a long story sort of short, I stumbled home a short distance from the bar where I rented a small hooch for my wife and me, and I found a bag of three large cans of green spray paint that I didn't need for an earlier Saint Patrick's Day celebration at our local Catholic school. I then drove over to our newly-expanded international airport and climbed over the security fence near runway 90 and hustled over to the runway about midnight. We didn't have too many daily commercial jet flights land at our small island's airport for our tourism industry, but one or two flights would land around midnight to bring many tourists from Japan. I hurriedly picked out an open area just past the runway's compass directional number 90 and painted a large and beautiful green shamrock on the airstrip for all our visiting pilots to see.

As I finished my green work of art in the runway darkness, suddenly the runway lit up like in the science fiction movies when a spaceship descends with a tremendous bright light shining all around. I quickly turned and saw the blinding landing lights of a Continental

Air Micronesian 727 directed my way since I was standing in the touchdown area for the jet.

After a quick piss in my pants I sprinted to the side of the runway and the jet landed. The vortex from jet's wings tossed me through the air and after a short gasp of "What the fuck?!" I ran over to the security fence and possibly leaped over it in a single bound and got in my truck and headed for Hamilton's

I arrived at Hamilton's and walked in with a frazzled state of mind and body. It was after midnight and all of Chief's patrons had left as I approached my regular place at the bar's open end and ordered two shots of tequila and a cold beer. Hamilton poured me my tequila and asked me where the hell had I been? Chief then noticed green paint sprayed all over my white tennis shoes and inquired about the half-ass paint job on my shoes. I said I would tell him later.

After thirty minutes or so, two Continental Air Micronesian pilots sauntered in and I quickly scooted through the bar's open end and into Hamilton's kitchen area and hid. The pilots knew Chief and would stop in for a nightcap before checking into their hotel rooms for their overnight layover. Soon I heard laughter when the pilots told Chief about a big green shamrock painted on the runway when they landed earlier, and they swore they saw some figure of a crazy son-of-a-bitch running off the airstrip in the glare of their landing lights. Chief was also laughing and said the guy probably had green shoes on for Saint Paddy's Day. The pilots did tell the Chief they had to report to the Saipan airport management so they could remove it later. But it did make for a good Saint Patrick's Saipan story for the pilots.

The tired pilots left after fifteen minutes and I came out from hiding in the kitchen. I made the Chief swear on our friendship and my promise to spend extra money in his bar to keep the green shoes a secret. He agreed and advise me to get rid of them and I tossed them in his trash can and walked home shoeless. I never got back to the Governor about his request for information on the runway paint job, and as I write this I wonder if the FAA could still nail me for the improper green landing aid I painted on Saipan's international airstrip.

James Bond-san Visits Saipan

Then there was the wild time I got the Governor to agree with me to allow a Japanese motion picture company to come to Saipan in early 1983 to make a goofy Japanese James Bond-type movie.

They wanted to shoot more than one-half of their frenetic version of the combination "James Bond" musical and adventure movie on Saipan. They had planned on shooting it on Guam, but Guam wanted too many government fees and costs to shoot the movie there.

So, the young Japanese producer, Ryu Murakami, and his location assistant, who was a talented white statesider, decided to visit my office and inquire if my boss, the Governor, would like to have a movie shot on Saipan.

The white location assistant, who used to work in Las Vegas as an Elvis impersonator and later connected with Murakami, came to me since I was the only white statesider working in the Governor's office at the time. Oh, lest I forget, we did have one other white statesider in the Governor's office, who was a good attorney but was always incapacitated with the "tropical flu," aka drunk, and he was mostly unavailable to do any special assignments for the Governor. So, I filled in whenever a white guy was needed for particular island white guy assignments.

The location assistant figured our small island governor would be more reasonable than the greedy "big island" Guamanian officials, and he was also banking on me, a fellow white guy, to pull it off.

Personally, I was all for it and knew the Governor would agree, too. Especially since our Governor liked action and western movies, and Peter Fonda was starring as the "James Bond" character. The movie company would also spend over two months on our island and spend a million or more dollars on the production.

In our meeting, the location assistant and Mr. Murakami told me that they didn't want to face highly prohibitive government costs to shoot the movie, nor did they want to apply and wait for a myriad of approvals from several government agencies.

After hearing about their problems with Guam, I told them to hang on while I called the Governor. I informed the Governor on the phone that we had a chance to make a real Hollywood-type movie here on Saipan if we cooperated with a wealthy Japanese producer who was in my office. The Governor sounded very interested, and I further enticed the Governor by saying that he could get a movie part, too.

After finishing my phone conversation with the Governor, the Japanese producer said the Governor wasn't planned to be in the movie but as a polite Japanese businessman, he shrugged and nodded okay to me. Meanwhile, I arranged a meeting to see the Governor in his office in thirty minutes.

The meeting went great, and I advised the Governor about all the problems the movie guys had on Guam with too many expensive government fees and the scheduling of long waits for shooting permits.

Luckily for the Japanese production team, the Governor agreed with my one-stop agency permit process and waiver of all fees. During the meeting, Murakami had said that the film company promised to spend a million plus dollars while shooting for about two months and, furthermore, that a hundred members of the Japanese press corps planned to visit Saipan while the movie was being made.

The Governor liked the idea that the Japanese press would provide our tourist island with free publicity while covering Peter Fonda, who was a major star in Japan after making the U.S. movie "Easy Rider." Fonda-san later got a large contract shooting motorcycle commercials in Japan.

So, it was a win-win for both parties. The CNMI's Saipan government would waive the fees in exchange for big movie production bucks and free tourist promotion to attract more tourists from our largest source of travelers in Japan. Besides, the Governor was going to have a part in the film, too!

The Governor had me immediately draft a letter for his signature that instructed all government agencies to not charge any fees or delay any shooting schedules. The Governor made me his liaison for the motion picture activities and to make sure that everything went smoothly as possible for the movie being shot on our island of Saipan.

The Japanese producer was amazed at his good fortune and soon called Japan and immediately scheduled reservations for everyone in his movie production company to fly on a JAL 747 jumbo jet to Saipan. The movie production team and equipment would be arriving in approximately ten days, including all the actors, crew, and media people to start shooting Ryu Murakami's convoluted "James Bond" musical movie.

The movie shoot became a great party for all of Saipan. It was very exciting and Saipan made a big splash in the tourism market, although Murakami's movie called "Daijobu (It's All Right), My Friend" wasn't a very successful movie at the box office.

The main problem was it apparently was Murakami's first attempt at moviemaking. In his novice attempt to make a big splash at the box office, he based his storyline on "James Bond," "Mr. Bean," "Superman," "E.T. The Extra-Terrestrial," "The Attack of the Killer Tomatoes," and the "Sound of Music."

I think it was an early lesson for Murakami in the art of how *not* to write a flop at the box office, but the fledgling producer went on to become a famous writer and movie producer in his later years.

Oh, yes, about the Governor's part in the movie. I read the script before they began shooting on Saipan and discovered there was some very explicit fully-naked scenes in the first part of the film that was previously shot on location in Japan. I had to warn the Governor about the nudity and cautioned him that the vast majority of the island voters on Saipan were Catholic. And as his trusted advisor most of the time, I warned him it might taint his own Catholic image being in a movie with stark-ass nudity.

The Governor reluctantly agreed and told me to tell the producer that I would help find a replacement for his part. I told the Governor I had already anticipated the problem and found a replacement.

He asked me who I found for his part and I just smiled. Yes, I was going to break into the movies and "star" alongside Peter Fonda! I even wrote some dialogue for my minor part and the director later accepted the lines. Yes, a speaking role in a movie with Peter Fonda-san!

I hoped the Governor wouldn't be upset that I grabbed his part, but he wisely understood that I didn't need the Catholic vote for my government position.

The Governor also reminded me to have fun but make sure I applied for an unpaid leave of absence for my money-making movie role, in order to avoid possible double dipping and the opposition party accusing the white guy of dastardly crimes and various misdemeanors.

The United Nations Bird Incident

Another unique and sensitive political adventure was the time I arranged our CNMI government's participation in a United Nations' (U.N.) Asian-Pacific meeting held at the U.N. ESCAP Headquarters in Thailand in September of 1983. I got everything planned for the trip and when the Governor signed the Travel Authorization (TA), he commented, "There's no traveler's name yet, who's going?"

I explained to the Governor that all his staff members were busy with the CNMI's special meeting with the TTPI entities, and I seemed to be the only one available. But I wanted to leave it up to him to make the final decision. The Governor smirked and asked, "The flight takes off soon, are you packed for the trip?"

"All ready to go, Governor." He told me to print my own name on the TA and get going to the airport.

At ESCAP, several of the major islands in the Asia-Pacific region (American Samoa, Western Samoa, the TTPI, etc.,) and other far east countries like Afghanistan, India, etc. all participated in the U.N.'s mission for Economic and Social Commission for Asia and the Pacific (ESCAP).

This particular meeting was tense since it happened soon after the Russians shot down a civilian jetliner, Korean Airlines Flight 007, killing all onboard. Russia's participation in ESCAP was also suspect because Russia really wasn't a regional part of the Asian-Pacific mission, but they had covert reasons to participate.

I arrived late on the first morning of the meeting and, since the ESCAP Assistant Secretary didn't have a nameplate and seat on the main floor for the Commonwealth of the Northern Mariana Islands (CNMI), he placed me in the Trust Territory of the Pacific Islands (TTPI) seat. This was right next to a mean-looking Russian official seated at the place of the Union of Soviet Socialist Republics (USSR).

Immediately, the Russian delegate challenged my being seated at a place that a Pacific islander would normally sit, not a tall, white-ass "American spy."

I had to submit my official documents showing I was actually representing my CNMI Governor, who had been officially invited by ESCAP and had approved my trip to the ESCAP meeting. I then loudly asked the Russian delegate, "Shot down any civilian planes lately?"

Well, the meeting was halted until there was an agreement that the Russian and I would play nice during the meeting.

The U.N. official photographer was then asked to take a picture of the Russian and me "smiling." The photograph was soon placed in the lobby to the chagrin of the Russian delegation. Then I got a lecture from the U.S. Ambassador to Thailand after an official protest was lodged against me for not playing nice during the photo op.

Apparently, the Thailand photographer didn't catch and/or comprehend the American hand signal I gave to the Russian in the photograph. I was giving him the all-American "flipping the bird" sign of "screw you" with my middle finger.

The Russian official did have me tailed and intimidated during the week-long session, but I ended up making friends with my likable and very large "Ruskie tail," who was a decent Russian just doing his job.

Once when I was cornered in the ESCAP elevator with the Ruskies, the Russian official told me the most important word I should understand in Russian is "Da," as in saying yes to their policies. I countered with the most important word that I knew in Russian was "Nyet," as in saying no to Russian intimidation. The Russian official snarled at me but the Russian tail behind him just smirked at my retort.

At least I made one Russian friend at ESCAP.

I also got the last diplomatic victory when I lobbied and got an insertion in our final ESCAP report, which criticized the Russians shooting down the KAL 007 and that Russia really didn't promote "positive" economic and social understanding in the Asia-Pacific region.

AAAAARRRRGGGGHHH!

Overall, my own positive attitude about working and interacting with people of color was dramatically improving during this time with the good Governor.

But my racial good vibes and diplomacy suddenly got short-circuited in June of 1985, when I fell victim to island politics and was abruptly replaced by an islander for political purposes, which even my friend the Governor could not prevent.

It started when I was called into a meeting prior to the Governor's reelection campaign. The meeting was held in the Governor's office, and it was attended by the Governor, his Special Assistant for Administration (SAA), who was a large and mean islander with a bad temper, and me the white guy.

The meeting's main topic was my being replaced by an islander, which would be more appreciated by the local island voters and which was being forced on the Governor by a temperamental and racist SAA.

The Governor tried to convince the SAA that I could be kept in the background while the local guy would handle my duties until after the election and then I would return to my position and the local guy would be given a nice cushy job somewhere else. As I earlier mentioned, the Governor was a great and gracious person who liked my loyalty, and my semi-screwy sensitive performance of my island duties.

However, during the meeting, the SAA became very angry about my holding a job that should belong to an islander. He started yelling at the Governor, and he did scare the Governor sometimes with his outbursts, e.g., he once tore his office and the outer Governor's lobby apart when he was refused an outlandish request of his, and we had to close the Governor's office until the damage was repaired. The SAA followed his latest outburst in our meeting by opening his briefcase, which was resting on his lap, and he pulled out a handgun and started waving it around like a mad man.

Of course, this quickly got the Governor's panicky attention, and he asked the SAA to please put the gun away, but the SAA just grinned like a maniac and kept waving his gun in the air and at me!

I had known about the SAA's penchant to scare people, mainly white statesiders, with his gun. So, subsequently, I quickly reached down and pulled my .38 caliber pistol from my adapted boot holster and began waving it around like the SAA was doing. It was the gun that the police had sold me earlier when I worked at the bowling center and some people had wondered why I wore uncomfortable bell-bottom pants and boots in the tropics, but it was a necessity for my stateside defense against threats by unhinged islanders, like the pissed-off SAA. It was also known that I had previously stated I would shoot back in any emergency involving my white butt being shot at by any of the less friendly island 30 percenters.

Now the Governor was looking at his two crazed staff members flashing weapons around in his office, and he quickly pleaded for us to calm down. The Governor then asked me to help him with the bad situation, and my being a friend of the Governor, I did relent and said I would resign for his benefit. The Governor then asked the SAA to leave the office, which he did, and I apologized to the Governor and he said he would somehow help me after I left my job.

Later on, I didn't blame the Governor for quickly accepting my resignation, but I was out of a job on an island that didn't have that many decent jobs for white-butt statesiders. AAAAARRRRGGGGHHH!

After losing my PIO job and not getting any government or non-government job offers partly due to the rumored story of a gun incident in the Governor's office, it became another rough patch in the tattered fabric of my life's adventures. Furthermore, my Palauan wife was not too happy about the jobless situation either.

However, by some unique twist of island fortune shortly thereafter, I began working for an influential local islander who owned a construction company.

As island karma would have it, he was in the opposition Democratic Party and he needed a statesider to write bid proposals for federal construction projects on the island. More importantly, I was informed by my wife that maybe I was going to be a papa for the first time at the ripe young age of 39.

My islander wife had previously suffered several miscarriages, but this pregnancy would hang on for a little over six months until early January 1986, when my wife suddenly rushed up to me while I was drinking at Hamilton's Bar. She was bleeding through the front of her jeans, and I was stunned and felt so sorry for my scared wife and ashamed that I was in a bar while she was battling to save our baby.

It was around six in the evening and we rushed to the small island hospital, but there was no doctor on duty to see my wife. I got word to the only Palauan doctor on island, and she came to the hospital just after midnight. She was a good young doctor and could speak in my wife's native Palauan language and it thankfully comforted her.

The doctor medicated my wife to slow down her body's attempt to expel our child, and then the doctor advised me that my wife needed to be placed on the first flight in the morning for an emergency medevac 120 miles away to the bigger island of Guam. Guam hospitals had better equipment with more medical specialists than Saipan.

But there were problems with the medevac procedure. Since it was 2 am in the morning, the medical referral staff were not available until 8 am and the medevac needed government approval.

By the time a request was made through "island government" channels, our baby could be lost. Such were the problems the island residents faced on our small and somewhat primitive island.

However, I had worked for our Governor and had arranged medevacs in the past, so I had connections with local hospital staff to get the ambulance ready for an early morning medevac.

When we finally located the local ambulance driver, he said he had to pick up his islander family with the ambulance later in the morning to go shopping (remember, this was a small island that had strange customs and priorities).

By 6 am, I had convinced the ambulance driver that it was an emergency and he saw my wife being wheeled out to the ambulance. A Palauan nurse and assistant began placing my medicated wife, who was secured in a gurney, into the ambulance, and I gave the local driver ten bucks. He liked the monetary inducement and decided to drive my wife and the nurse to the airport before his family's shopping trip.

I rushed home, which was near the airport, to get my U.S. passport and my wife's special U.S. temporary passport until her permanent passport arrived later. Even though it was a medevac, we would need these to enter Guam.

We all met at the airport in good time, and I then talked to the small commuter airline supervisor and informed him that this was an emergency medevac and that the government paperwork would arrive later.

Since I had helped the commuter airline's management several times in the past with medevacs, which were handled by the commuter airline that had a government contract, the supervisor believed my story about the approval paperwork arriving later and my wife and the nurse would be soon headed for Guam.

There was no room for me in the small plane, so I flew on a departing 727 commercial jet and arrived before my wife. I was cleared by U.S. Immigration on Guam, which inanely insisted on checking Saipan arrivals even though Saipan was a part of a U.S. commonwealth. Fortunately, I got permission to nervously stand on the tarmac waiting for the Guam Hospital ambulance for my scared wife.

The emergency medevac flight had already called from the air to the Guam Airport Tower and it was relayed to the hospital to immediately send an ambulance.

The ambulance soon arrived and the small medevac plane finally landed and parked on the tarmac near the waiting ambulance. The Guam Hospital's ambulance attendants hastily headed toward the plane and placed my wife on the gurney because the special medication for her and the baby was wearing off and they needed to get to the hospital pronto.

However, an unsmiling U.S. Immigration Officer on Guam, who was an arrogant Guamanian islander, stopped my wife's gurney and asked to see her valid I.D. to enter Guam. I urgently showed the officer my wife's U.S. temporary passport, but he incredibly refused to accept the I.D. until she filled out a convoluted I-94 form for people of Palauan descent.

Meanwhile, the hospital doctor was yelling over the ambulance radio to get the patient to the hospital immediately. I guess my mind snapped with the ongoing ludicrous situation causing my struggling wife and unborn child to be dangerously delayed on the hot airport tarmac by an asinine islander immigration officer. So, I grabbed the officer, pinned him to the ground, and yelled to the ambulance attendants to leave immediately.

Everyone was initially stunned by my actions, and even my wife called out for me to stop or I would be arrested. But I yelled that our baby's trip to the hospital was more important than my being arrested for beating the hell out of a stupid immigration official.

After hearing the Guam hospital doctor shout again on the ambulance radio, the ambulance attendants realized I wasn't going to let the immigration officer get up, so they hurriedly loaded my wife in the ambulance and departed for the hospital.

Later, I was released from airport detention when the Director of U.S. Immigration Services on Guam heard what happened and checked the hospital about the condition of my wife. The director was told that it would be very helpful for me to be at the hospital to support my wife who was scared about losing another baby.

So, the immigration director, who was a no-nonsense white guy, had me brought to his office and released me on the condition that I surrender my passport and my wife's special U.S. temporary passport. He also instructed me to report back to his office later after the emergency at the hospital was under control. He wished me and my wife good luck with the baby and I rushed to the hospital to tearfully and fortunately witness the birth of our premature baby girl in the delivery room.

I got to hold my precious little fighter and then she had to be placed in an incubator. After a few days, our baby girl would be ready to go home to Saipan.

However, I had to first report to the office of the U.S. Director of Immigration in order to find out my punishment for assaulting an immigration jerk on the airport tarmac.

The director met with me in his office and said he was happy that everything was okay with my wife and baby. He then stated that after he reviewed witness statements from several people at the scene of the incident, he informed me that I acted in a "justifiable" manner under the conditions.

He returned my U.S. passport and my wife's U.S. temporary passport, which the director declared was a proper U.S. I.D. to enter Guam. Next, he informed me that he had reprimanded the immigration officer for a grievous action of delaying a medical emergency without any rightful cause. He asked if I planned to file any action against the immigration officer and his office. I replied that I made a promise to the Good Lord, that if my baby survived, I would take my wife and baby back home to Saipan as soon as possible and try to forget the stupidity of the arrogant Guamanian immigration officer.

The director then had the asshole immigration officer come into the office to apologize to me for his uncalled-for actions, which could have resulted in a medical tragedy. At the sight of him, I lost it again and lurched toward him, still angered by his stupid actions. The director shouted for me to stop, and I did. I then left the office saying nothing. But bless the Lord, I was a new papa!

Later, Governor Tenorio became my daughter's godfather at her baptism, which was a true sign of island friendship I had with the Governor who included my daughter in his traditional family circle.

As a matter of record, when the hospital contacted me for an "unauthorized" medevac to Guam and presented me with a staggering bill of over three thousand dollars for the medevac trip and hospital care, I said send the bill to my daughter's godfather. I was never contacted about the bill again. My family was given a break by the island gods and my former boss, the good Governor Pedro P. Tenorio.

Since becoming a father, the local gods seemed to bless me and the CNMI government's public school system finally hired me in the fall of 1986 to be an English teacher at the only public junior high school on Saipan. The school system was short on stateside teachers with any type of college degree to teach English classes. It was a known fact that the local islanders wanted any white stateside English teacher, who had a pulse and wasn't a habitual drunk, to teach their children basic English proficiency to get qualified for the federally-sponsored jobs, which were becoming more available with the extra federal funding that kept pouring into the local coffers.

Regrettably, for the mostly xenophobic islanders, the number of white folks was increasing now on Saipan, due to the need for stateside teachers and other statesiders to help the politically naïve islanders to discover the various ways to the federal vault.

And more regrettable for the islanders, most of the newly arrived white statesiders were semi-zombie drifters, who were mostly zonked out on booze and drugs, except me of course, who just had a few beers and an "occasional" tequila shooter or two whenever the sun went down or when I sometimes stayed too long in the tropical sun without a hat.

Thank goodness that my tropical education career got a later boost when I was also admitted into a Master of Arts program that would be taught on Saipan by stateside instructors from San Jose State University.

My master's degree in the summer of 1989 later helped me get a surprise promotion to become the first white vice principal at Saipan's only public high school, Marianas High School. At the time, most local islander educators had not yet attained a master's degree to become educational administrators, which was needed to support the high school in getting its U.S. accreditation.

Moreover, I had local support for the vice principal's job from the sympathetic indigenous Carolinians on the public school board, partly because I was ably raising a Carolinian (Palauan) little girl by myself. Furthermore, I got a much-needed raise to cover my parental expenses and secure a very pleasant live-in Filipina maid to help me with my little girl.

Previously, due to certain island eccentricities that were out of my control, my Palauan wife became disenchanted at being a mother and had decided that she wanted to experience the big island life of Hawaii and, as a mutually agreeable result, we amicably split and I kept our one-year-old daughter. Wow, at age forty, I finally had to really grow up and be a single parent.

But just before my wife left in the spring of 1987, I had a very unique island experience when I visited Hamilton's Bar and it could have derailed my educational career on Saipan. I had gone into Hamilton's to solve some local and world problems and to also ask Hamilton about the challenges of being married to an island woman, who had very different ways of looking at life than a white statesider.

Hamilton was an ex-Navy Chief Petty Officer during World War II, and he stayed in the islands after the war and married a nice island lady. They had their differences, especially when Chief drank too much Canadian Club and got into funny arguments with his wife, but they somehow stayed together.

Chief Hamilton tried to explain that some marriages with island ladies just don't work out and you have to move on. I agreed and didn't get stupid drunk that night, and I left around 10 pm to go home to deal with a strained relationship. I wanted the last days of my marriage to be peaceful.

However, while hastily driving on the way home, I was not focusing on the dark narrow road near Hamilton's and forgot about an old coconut tree that had fallen over partly into the road on an inclined angle. It created a sort of an upward ramp in front of me and, being slightly inebriated, I unwittingly sped up the tree ramp and went airborne and turned upside down as I crashed back onto the road and went scrapping along on the truck's roof.

Next, there was a sudden stoppage of my upside-down truck and since I wasn't wearing my seat belt, I was launched through the front window and rolled to a stop on my back looking up at the spinning stars.

A local couple ran out of their nearby house and asked if I was okay. I mumbled something and they helped me to my feet. I then uttered I was going back to Hamilton's Bar to get help to move my truck out of the road, and the couple said they would watch over the accident scene until the police arrived.

Soon thereafter, I stumbled barefoot into Hamilton's with visible cuts and abrasions all over my body since I was only wearing jogging shorts and a ripped t-shirt. My flip-flops were also missing from my feet. I had bits of glass in my hair, and some were stuck to my face and shirt. Chief Hamilton was drinking a big glass of Canadian Club and coke and blurted out, "What the hell happened to you?"

I tried to explain my poor execution of a flying daredevil stunt with my truck and then I noticed that Chief didn't have any customers to help me move my truck, due to the fact it had been a slow night at the bar.

Chief slurred that I looked like I needed a drink and gave me the half-filled bottle of Canadian Club and I drank the entire contents. After about fifteen minutes, I suddenly blurted out that I needed to move my truck and wobbled out of the bar.

When I approached the scene of my coconut tree accident, there were several police cars and a fire truck surrounding my truck with their red lights flashing, along with a few flood lights lighting up the whole area.

The police officers were looking in and around my truck and then they saw me staggering toward them. They had found my registration and they recognized me from my days working at the governor's office. Most of them were friendly, but a few officers were upset that I had left the scene of the accident to conceal that I was driving drunk. They also said that I foolishly abandoned my truck sitting upside down in the middle of the road and they proceeded to handcuff my hands in front of my body.

Meanwhile, a nearby car repair shop owner had been rousted out of bed by the police and had already hooked a cable to the truck. The truck was starting to be flipped over with help from some cooperating officers. I tried to help but struggled with my being handcuffed and slipped to the road in a drunken heap.

The truck was removed and the car repair shop owner said to me that he would fix the scrapes and dents on the truck and replace the broken windshield.

I mumbled, "Okay," while still sitting on the road. I knew he was a good Filipino repairman and had a reputation to fix things and not overcharge.

I was then placed into one of the officer's cars by an agitated islander officer who said I would be spending the night in jail. So much for my attempt to go home to keep peace with my soon-departing wife.

It turned out that the night jailer was a friend of mine and he let me out of my cell around 4 am. He kindly took me home as an island favor, since he knew I had to show up for work at school at 7:30 am.

After arriving home, my wife and I didn't talk at all and she left the following day for Hawaii. I honestly didn't think too much about her departure since I had to take care of my little girl. I had to further find a day maid to care for my daughter while I worked at school and attended a special master's degree program taught on island in the afternoons.

For the time being, I brought my well-behaved little girl to school and my classes, which was an acceptable custom in the islands in an emergency, and she was well-received by my students and the visiting college professors from the U.S. mainland.

I soon found a very nice Filipina day maid and life, work, and school were going okay, until two months later when I was dragged into court for the offense of driving under the influence and for damaging a culturally honored coconut tree. This court matter could create a big problem for my educational career, so I gathered my "team" to defend myself from charges filed by an irate islander cop and prosecutor who both claimed I had disrespected the island's tranquility by sailing upside down the road and leaving the scene of a serious accident, in order to cowardly conceal my high level of intoxication.

I was appointed a public defender, who was a recently graduated local attorney who got a degree by mail with a minimal amount of law courses. Of course, he passed the island bar test that was administered by I think one of his uncles.

The case opened with a barrage of accusations against my poor judgment and drunken display while driving on a peaceful residential island road. My island reputation was shredded by the government prosecutor and lengthy testimony by the irate local officer who I had a suspicion that he really disliked white statesiders. He must have been a "thirty percenter" and gave damning testimony about my lengthy ticket citation and criminal report in great biased detail.

It was now my public defender's turn to cross-examine the officer. He stood up and stammered, "No questions, your honor."

"What!" I cried out and I respectfully asked the judge, who seemed to be a considerate and mellow island judge, if I could cross-examine the office myself.

The judge replied, "Go ahead," since he knew my attorney, his nephew, was very nervous and it was his first case that he was handling in open court. I got up and tried to draw upon my memories of TV lawyers in the states, approached the police officer, and asked him if he would swear on a stack of bibles and his own family and his temperamental mother-in-law that he witnessed my driving drunk.

The church-going officer thought about swearing on the stack of bibles but felt much more stress thinking about the possible backlash from his mother-in-law and stammered that he actually didn't see me driving drunk. Although he explained that the circumstantial evidence of my staggering upon the scene to check on my truck was enough evidence to either hang me or toss me to the sharks.

I ended my cross-examination by having the officer state under the threat of perjury (and an angry scolding from his mother-in-law) that he, in fact, did not see me driving under the influence.

The police officer was excused and, since he was the only witness for the prosecution, the judge asked if I had any evidence or witnesses to present to the court. I looked at my nervous lawyer and asked him if I could continue defending myself. He quickly agreed, and I proceeded to advise the court and the prosecution of my two witnesses.

My first witness was the local neighbor who was first on the scene and saw me lying on the road. I asked him if I was drunk. He said I appeared a little wobbly from the result of flying through my windshield, but that I appeared coherent enough to say that I was going back to Hamilton's Bar to ask for help to move my truck. He also said I had asked him to watch my truck and help any traffic to drive around it. He further said that he had a flashlight at the time and he remembered shining it in my face and stated that I didn't look drunk, but just sort of shaken up from my accident, which he figured was caused by the coconut tree dangerously sticking out in the road.

The witness then partly blamed the government for the accident because he had asked the government's road maintenance crew to remove the tree several times, but no one had taken any action for months.

Feeling cocky with the positive local support of my defense argument, I asked him if he thought that the government work schedules were possibly delayed by lazy island road workers. Furthermore, I suggested that if the witness offered a case of cold beer to the island road workers, maybe the coconut tree would have been removed in only a week or two.

My witness, not seeking the wrath of island government workers, really didn't want to answer my question and the judge interrupted the proceedings and advised me to not criticize the government workers, probably because the judge was related to most of them on such a small island. I then realized I was entering into a danger zone of a wise-ass white outsider offending the culturally sensitive acceptance of delayed government work and that it was a time-honored island privilege to procrastinate. I quickly apologized to the judge and offered a general apology to any possible upset government road worker who could take a front loader and push my recently repaired truck into the Saipan lagoon.

My next witness was Chief Hamilton, who said in my defense that I wasn't drunk when I arrived at his bar after the accident, but sure in hell was drunk after he had given me a bottle of Canadian Club and I had quickly guzzled a half quart of his favorite booze. The Chief then said that I had staggered out of his bar to go back to my truck to see what I could do. The Chief finished his testimony by asking his friend the judge to stop by his bar again, which got a few chuckles from the people in the courtroom.

What happened next was my best "Perry Mason" closing argument. Professional court procedures and rules were not really followed at this island-style trial, so I directly addressed the judge since this was a bench trial (no jury). I stated this was not a case of driving under the influence or DUI, but a clear case of walking under the influence, or WUI.

Therefore, I should be fined only for public drunkenness, and since every night most of the population of men on the island were drunk due to public boredom, I finally asked for the court's mercy to spare me a DUI or a WUI, which could jeopardize my school job and seriously affect my supporting my little girl as a single parent. I also promised that I wouldn't drive up a culturally sacred coconut tree ever again.

The judge agreed with my cockeyed line of reasoning and dismissed both the DUI and WUI charges. He did fine me five dollars for having no license in my possession on the night of the accident.

But in my defense, I explained that a government worker, who was assigned to clean up the mess I made with the coconut tree, had found my missing wallet under some bushes by the road accident. I argued that I had my license that night, but it went sailing out of my jogging shorts sometime during my own flying escapade out of my truck. I also lamented that I received only one of my lost flip-flops.

The judge seriously looked at me and said, "I'll offer you a choice of giving you a hundred-dollar fine for public drunkenness or a five-dollar fine for having no license in your possession while being arrested for public mayhem. What will it be?"

I quickly took out my battered wallet and tried to hand the judge a five-dollar bill. He smiled and instructed me to give it to his clerk.

Favorable tropical justice can do one's soul some real good during the surreal times of one's island trials and tribulations.

Getting back to my earlier times at Marianas High School, I did okay as vice principal on Saipan, and it got me "promoted" in 1990 to the outer island of Tinian. There, I would be the only white principal in the public school system. It involved the administration of an out-of-control small high school that didn't even have a 12th grade.

Right before leaving for tiny Tinian Island, I also got married again to a young Filipina lady who fearlessly said she was willing to move with me to the little and rowdy Tinian Island from the bigger and safer island of Saipan. Well, that seemed workable to have a "fighter" at my side for any upcoming combat action.

The Tinian High School's principal's job was open because no islander educator on Tinian or Saipan wanted the wild and dangerous job. During a previous school administrators' meeting on Saipan, where I was then the only white administrator (vice principal) in the public school system, it was joked, "Why not give the brutal job to the white guy?"

I impulsively said to myself, "Why not, it pays more, as long as I can survive the outer island ambivalence toward anyone with the distinct color of ivory soap."

As it turned out, all the local island administrators on Saipan deviously agreed to my agreeing for the educational combat duty on Tinian. They figured that this would teach an uppity white boy a good lesson on a tiny isolated outer island, where it would be difficult for me to hide from any islander who really didn't care for an ivory-soap-looking statesider.

Later, after I arrived on Tinian, most of the local 1200 islanders there went totally nuts when they actually realized an anxious white guy was occupying their high school principal's office.

Frankly, the next two years were pretty much small island crazyville, and the only way to battle a semi-crazy racial environment on an isolated miniature island was being a semi-crazy outsider who tried to keep a few steps ahead of the locals.

Moreover, as a nice distraction from the continuous Tinian mayhem, I was further blessed with a beautiful baby boy. But again and similar to my daughter's birth, my son's birthing process was fraught with potential danger.

My wife had to be hurriedly placed on a medevac to Saipan for our baby's birth for lack of a doctor on Tinian. This was due to the presence of only a semi-educated local "medical officer" at the small Tinian Health Clinic, and he couldn't deliver babies, let alone treat a pimple on someone's ass. This situation was due to an earlier and very abrupt departure of the only certified doctor on Tinian. The doctor was an unfortunate white statesider, who was seriously threatened and attacked by some local thugs needing excessive amounts of prescription painkillers.

My wife and our baby survived the short plane ride to the main hospital on Saipan, and damn, I was a proud papa again. Although there was one serious problem with our little boy. He was born with a severe cleft palate condition and island discrimination against Filipina mothers prevented a U.S. ENT (ear, nose, and throat) specialist to see our baby for corrective surgery in the not-too-distant future.

The ENT doctor was flown every six months to Saipan from the U.S. mainland, in order to provide the necessary ENT support and surgery for island children and young adults. Even though our boy had me as a U.S. father, the local hospital nursing staff wrote "Filipino baby" on his chart, which I later discovered, and the ENT doctor was only scheduled for U.S. island residents, not Filipino babies.

Later, I resolved this issue myself due to my own method of managing tropical madness and the kind help of the island gods who possessed indirect methods of blessing unprotected outsiders.

To recap some of my "Principal of Paradise" adventures on Tinian, the following is a list of various unorthodox actions and strategies that I undertook in order to convince the indigenous residents of Tinian that they were dealing with a wily whitey, who was possibly sent by the gods to even the playing field in paradise. I was going to write a short book called "Principal of Paradise," but the following should suffice and save me from hours of toil while sitting on my ass and aggravating my aging hemorrhoids.

The Gang of Nine

During my initial meeting with the Tinian High School (THS) student body, I spoke about the state of the high school's reputation. The total high school student population numbered around 120 students since it didn't have a twelfth grade due to the lack of 12th-grade teachers, who didn't want to leave the bigger and less dangerous island of Saipan. The high school was also not accredited due to its erratic and dysfunctional administration of both the unruly students and parents. I promised that I would change the poor environment of the school with the students' help and the help of the teachers and parents---I truly hoped and prayed.

I had also promised I would fix the lack of a 12th grade and I did the very first month of the school year. I had a supply of 12th-grade textbooks, and I had earlier recruited some unfairly treated Saipan stateside teachers who all had 12th-grade teaching experience in all the necessary subject areas, except English. Since I had the experience, I would teach 12th grade English class and be the THS principal too. I officially created the first THS 12th grade and all the parents of 12th grade students, who had to send their sons and daughters to Saipan to attend 12th grade, were ecstatic. The Public School System (PSS) and its arrogant Commissioner of Education always considered THS a loser of a high school, which would never get organized enough to get a 12th grade or ever become accredited. But we did create a successful 12th grade that would someday lead us to future accreditation.

During my first meeting with the THS student body, I noticed nine 11th-grade punks casually sitting in the back of the small auditorium and jeering at my short motivational speech. I subsequently asked the more behaved students if they felt the school would be better off without the very disruptive male students in the back. Due to the island custom of always supporting their own island people over white outsiders, they seemed to be non-committal until a few of the female students started complaining about the nine punks in the back and their shit-for-brains attitude.

Soon, these few female students were joined by other fed-up students and challenged me about what I could do to remedy the situation. Being an outsider on their xenophobic island and also being very white, I paused for a moment, and then a remedy did strike me from the heavens.

I immediately announced that the nine punks were hereby expelled for their repulsive and contemptuous attitudes and they would have to individually meet me in my office with their parents, guardians, or parole officers to sign a contract to grow up and become better students. They would also not bother the remaining student body with their disruptive behaviors anymore. The punks were stunned and threatened me as I escorted them out of the auditorium and locked the door.

The next week was quite challenging and a near disaster for my physical health as irate parents and relatives bombarded my office with threats and all sorts of mayhem. One island thug of a father even spat in my face. I was being patient until that spit hit my face and then I went ballistic. I wanted to leap over my desk and jump on the bastard spitter. I didn't really care about being fired in my first month as principal at a high school from tropical hell. I counted to about four to bring my anger down a few notches and then angrily knocked everything off my desk in a fit of rage. The stunned parent thought I had flipped out and quickly left my office, muttering, "Fucking crazy outsider."

Nothing more came about it and it was just added to the continuously growing list of Tinian acts of bat-shit-crazy small island antics.

During the same time of the spit and shit principal situation, I had several other parents of the female students support me because of the high rate of student pregnancies, which were mostly caused by the out-of-control high school macho dysfunction predator sex maniacs. I also held my ground and all nine punks reluctantly signed contracts and surprisingly, they all somehow became decent students with only "minor" negative incidents in the future.

Rule 1 & Rule 2

One of the minor negative incidents from the "Gang of Nine Punks" was that the punks had always worn their baseball hats in class. I had only two rules for classroom behavior, i.e., Rule 1) Don't do it, and Rule 2) Read Rule Number 1 again.

I felt that students should know what the basic school rules are by the time they reached high school, so I wanted to keep it simple for them.

Anyway, during one of my early observation visits to the classrooms, I needed to check on the teachers' classroom management methods.

My current crop of teachers was a little bit shaky and mostly semi-alcoholic white male statesiders, along with some hard-working Filipina teachers. All the ex-Saipan teachers had recently quit or been reprimanded and/or unfairly terminated. As a PSS principal, I had the authority to hire whoever was available, and even with the dangerous reputation of Tinian High School and all previous outsider teachers quitting Tinian due to its wild reputation, my current and "valiant" group of ex-Saipan teachers all decided to come with me to Tinian because I had a pressing emergency of having only two Tinian teachers at the time and, luckily, the ex-Saipan teachers all needed jobs and all agreed to come to Tinian from Saipan after I promised them support, safety, and a small raise since as principal I also had the power to justifiably boost their salaries.

While checking one particular classroom, I noticed that a few members of the "Gang of Nine Punks" were wearing hats. I entered the room and stopped the class. I politely informed the hat violators of the Public School System (PSS) dress code rules for students and I said I thought it showed better PSS manners to not wear hats inside the classroom. I further stated that I had no problem with students wearing hats outside in the tropical sun.

My short and sweet request for the punk members to take off their hats was met with menacing stares and one punk telling me to take a hike off a nearby ocean cliff. I promptly confiscated their hats and told the students to pick them up in my office in two days.

After school, the few hatless punks angrily came into my office and demanded their hats back immediately. I had fortunately hired an ex-Marine as a part-time English teacher and office assistant who worked at a desk in the corner of my office. He walked over next to me and I informed the students they would have to come through my office assistant and me to get their hats that were sitting on a shelf behind me. The student punks pondered their chances of overcoming two rather intimidating white guys and then swore at us. I said those were profane "hat infraction comments" and that I would keep the hats for another week. They abruptly left the office saying they would get me later. Some students are such lovely young people.

Aren't Principals Allowed to Fight Back?

The same evening of the "hat infraction" incident, I was coming out of a small island store holding my five-year-old mixed ethnic island daughter, when out of the dark and rainy night, I was quickly approached by three pissed-off hatless punks who yelled they were going to kick my white ass.

Fortuitously, one of my white teachers was with me and I tossed my daughter into his arms. I then proceeded to leap on all three students and it was a wild melee in the muddy parking lot. I don't think the punks knew I had played rough-and-tumble college football at Washington State University in the U.S. mainland and loved a good melee.

We eventually called a joint truce, as one of the punks amusingly said that school principals are not supposed to fight students. I informed the student that this principal was somewhat "different," especially when I was carrying my young child who was exposed to danger.

Later that night after midnight, my wife and I were rudely awakened by a loud car driving wildly around the large front yard of our house and by screaming shouts of anger. I looked out a front window as my young daughter ran up to me and appeared scared at the loud voices and all the racket outside. I told my daughter to join her (step)mother and brother in our bedroom while I investigated this assault on our privacy.

I then went to the side door, grabbed my machete, and stripped naked. I was ready for crazy combat with some disturbed locals, probably related to the hatless punks, who wanted to harass and scare my family. My next move was a combination of sheer stupidity and bravado, as I went outside chasing the car and yelling war chants. The two occupants of the car seemed startled at this screaming white-like naked ghost chasing them with a swinging machete and the car suddenly drove off.

I eventually went back inside and quickly put my boxer shorts and t-shirt back on, in order to not alarm my wife who finally came out to see if I was okay. I really didn't want my wife to see my earlier nude combat attire so she wouldn't freak out that she had married a certifiable wacky white warrior.

The following day, I was in the island mayor's office explaining my fight incident with students. I told him I had to stand up to the island riff-raff or I would be run off the island with my tail between my legs. Furthermore, I explained that I defended my island daughter's well-being and would not apologize for the incident. I told him that he could have my resignation since the Tinian mayor was the political top dog on the island and could kick anybody off his island.

The mayor said that he knew that I was a good friend of his late father and that everything was okay because he said it was an island custom to protect anyone's family at any cost. When I left his office, he did ask me about a weird report of a naked white man chasing some local residents in the early morning hours. I shrugged and said I didn't know anything about that, but I would get back to him if I did hear something.

The mayor just smiled and I said goodbye. I had earlier discovered that the locals loved it when "any island resident" did goofy things while living on an island that had a serious lack of social entertainment.

The same day at school, I noticed that I was being admired by several students for standing up against the punks. So slowly I was gaining some positive island credibility. The other good thing was that the wild escapades on Tinian were normally ignored by the education officials on Saipan who considered them rumors or typical behavior of Tinian residents who had nothing better to do but get seriously drunk and get into "mischief." I do have to honestly admit that my own drinking had risen a few notches since my arrival on Tinian.

King Arthur's Hats

The final act of the hat wars was when I announced about a week later to the student body—via the morning public intercom announcements—that the students who had their hats confiscated by me earlier could get them at the new volleyball court at the mid-morning break time.

Unbeknownst to the hatless punks, I had poured cement in the holes for the volleyball court poles the evening before with the help of my ex-Marine office assistant, and I had stuck the hats in the cement with only the bills of the caps sticking out. I left a small sign next to the hats saying they could have their hats if they could pull them out of the cement, like in the story about the King Arthur legend and pulling out the sword from the stone.

During the break time, a large crowd of students gathered around the punks who stared at their hats in the cement and, eventually, they all laughed at my crazy retaliatory stunt to teach the hatless punks a "historical" King Arthur lesson. Hey, I'm supposed to be an educator, right?

The Rambo Knife Incident

The following story of one particular student needs special mention as one of my top "troubled young males" in my educational career. The fifteen-year-old student—I won't reveal his name since he was a minor at the time—was sort of weird and paranoid about his social position in life. He was fighting serious mental issues, caused by his messing around with some of his father's meth drug supply and being recently dumped by his girlfriend who was nervous about his escalating paranoia.

One morning, a student ran into my office, shouting, "A student is holding all of Miss A's science class hostage and has a big fucking knife!" My first reaction was to counsel the young student about the use of profane language in the sanctity of my prestigious small island school office, but my reaction time to the real problem at hand was slightly delayed by my periodic listless mind, which sometimes languished in a tropical zombie mode.

The emergency lightbulb immediately went off between my ears and I hastily headed for the science classroom trying to formulate a plan of action, after I had first called our lazy and inefficient police headquarters to help handle the situation. Then I realized the tropical cops would take an hour to reach the high school campus, even though their main office was across the dirt road from our school.

So, when getting close to the science classroom, I quietly crept up to a window of the crime scene and noticed that the student maniac had the class of twelve students and Miss A crowded in a corner of the classroom. He was waving a large Rambo-style knife, which belonged to his father for farm use to skin pigs, cows, etc., but now I hoped it wouldn't be used to skin a freaked-out student or Miss A!

I slowly entered the classroom while the students distracted the knife-wielding student with their pleas of don't hurt us. I eventually got between the disturbed student and his captives. The student suddenly lunged at me and I jumped back. I finally convinced the student to come outside with me so he could vent his anger toward me—the whitey-looking principal. The Rambo student agreed, thinking it would be better to have a white principal crap in his pants than poor Miss A, who was a small white female who at the time probably wished she was teaching at a small farm community school in Iowa.

The student and I got outside and, as I began my plea for the agitated student to calm down, he thrust the knife toward my neck and I quickly grabbed it by the blade as it slightly sliced my neck. Wow! This was getting surreal, and my half-Sicilian and half-Norwegian bloodlines instantly brought on survival tactics fostered by Eric the Red and the famous Mafia Godfather Marlon Brando.

I took my other hand and grabbed the student's hand on the knife handle, and using my extra adrenaline-pumped strength, I twisted the knife back toward the student's neck. I then shouted in his face, "One of us is probably going to die, and it ain't gonna be me, you little prick!"

The sudden shock of being overpowered by a large pissed-off principal made the student drop to his knees and let go of the knife. Right on island time, an old rusty island police car sputtered to the scene, about thirty minutes after I called the police headquarters. This fat-ass island cop finally got out of the car and pulled his fucking gun on me, since I was holding the knife now and the student was on his knees.

Thankfully, a few students ran out and told the cop what was going on, and the cop eventually took the student to the police station.

Fifteen minutes later, I was called to the station to give my statement. The student's father, who was a bad news drug dealer, was there, and we all had an island pow-wow on how to handle the situation. It was revealed that the student's mother was in Hawaii fighting cancer and that he had a bad breakup with his girlfriend. The Chief of Police finally asked if I wanted to press charges, but I just recommended that the student stay at his father's farm, which was outside of our main village, and I would provide him with his school lessons and arrange visits with our school's part-time counselor, who was an old and very wise islander.

After two weeks went by, the counselor said the student was ready to return and he was back in school. The student seemed okay as I kept a wary eye on him, and sure enough, a few days later, someone jabbed holes with a screwdriver through the radiator of my truck. I had to buy a used radiator and I then noticed that the previous knife-wielding student was giving me weird smiles. I had a feeling he was sneaking into his father's meth supply again and he still harbored deep-down feelings of dislike for me for making him lose face in front of the other students.

Losing face, or getting embarrassed in front of your island friends, was a touchy subject in the islands, and getting revenge was guaranteed at some time in the future to gain back some "face." My Sicilian-Norwegian "face" genealogy kicked in again and I inherently possessed an "anti-losing face" factor, too.

A week later, on a moonless night after midnight, I put on my "combat fatigues" and crawled military style into the house compound of the radiator-stabbing student's large family compound. They had dogs to protect the father's meth/drug operation, so I brought plenty of cans of Vienna sausages and tossed them all around the property away from the troubled student's prized shiny vehicle. I had only a few minutes for my principal military mission because the dogs were devouring the sausages in record time. I commenced to puncture all the student's tires with my Filipina wife's favorite fish filet knife and then I quickly crawled and ran through a dark muddy field filled with thorny bushes.

I eventually got home looking like shit, and my wife was awake and waiting for me to come home after she had previously noticed I was not in bed with her or anywhere in the house. I took off all my dirty clothes and winced at the thorn pricks on my arms and face. I then handed my wife's favorite knife to her that was bent and partially broken. She attempted to get a lucid explanation from me about my midnight madness and her broken knife, but I told her she wouldn't comprehend the deep retaliatory measures of a Mafia-Viking white principal who had to take on paradise to keep his face or credibility or whatever. She resigned herself not to dig deeper into the mind of a semi-crazed white guy trying to survive on a small tropical island, but she did insist that I had to buy her a damn new fish filet knife.

The next day at school, the "troubled student" nervously asked my secretary to see me and she let him into my office. He was shaken, paranoid, and incoherent from taking too much meth. He kept telling me that someone was after him because his father was dealing drugs. I inquired what had happened to make him so agitated. He said some son of a bitch stabbed his car and it can't move. I sarcastically asked him how could a person stab his car since it was made out of metal? He then stammered the assassin stabbed all his tires and he found empty cans of Vienna sausages all over the place. I acted surprised that such a diabolical act was committed, and I also warned him that maybe it was a sign that he needed to get off the meth and become a better person. He began muttering to himself and left my office.

Two days later, his father was busted for drug dealing by the Department of Justice boys, who were tipped off on Saipan and, subsequently, the FBI flew over to Tinian and busted three local guys, including the student's father. As a result, the student did a backflip into deep repentance and told me later that the tire-stabbing and his dad getting busted were serious signs from God. Yeah, a sign from God and from a retaliatory reaction of a pissed-off principal who had to buy an expensive used radiator for his old but prized truck and a new kitchen knife for his wife.

Oh yeah, I almost forgot to mention that in the next principals' meeting with our vain and pompous local Commissioner of Education, he accused me of illegally confiscating a local student's private property (the big fucking Rambo knife) without due process and he was thinking of suspending me. I blurted out that the knife was part of a serious hostage situation and I also got a cut on my neck as a reminder of the white man's peril on an isolated small Pacific island that housed some pretty sociopathic local islanders.

Furthermore, I had reluctantly given the knife back to the student's drug-dealing father, who recently had been arrested by the feds, and I didn't even press charges against the troubled student because his mother was seriously ill in Hawaii.

But being the only white principal in the meeting and having made some anti-local statements about island sociopaths, led to some biased and racist discussions that the local principals should support the local Commissioner against me.

Fortunately for me, one local principal who was a Carolinian islander—Carolinians were uniquely different than the other indigenous island Chamorro inhabitants—finally came to my rescue and said that I had a right to defend myself, even though I was an outsider. She also commended me for having compassion for the student and his family.

My final defense for my actions was, that when students' safety was involved, I didn't care what color the participants possessed, and I was going to quickly and prudently act as the leader of the school. I also was not going to think about any civil rights cockamamie, or any other inappropriate and inane personal rights theories that stupid sociologists preached, which would invariably tie a principal's hands together in an emergency.

I got a few nods of approval but then the Commissioner, who still wanted me punished, complained that he had also heard a rumor that I had drunkenly attacked a few students in a store's parking lot some time ago. No one really commented about that, just thinking it was another zany rumor on Tinian and, thankfully, we ended our meeting without me being banished from my principal's position.

Betel Nut Wars

The strange but sacred use in the islands of chewing betel nut, which is the size of a small walnut, was something an outsider had to accept, even if it meant the islanders would spit stinky red juice all over the place. Chewing the semi-narcotic betel nut is an island art form that is cherished by young and old in the Pacific islands. It involves splitting a betel nut in half, sprinkling a limestone powder on the inside, then closing the nut and wrapping it with a piece of pepper leaf. You add extra buzz to the concoction by breaking off a piece of a cigarette and sticking that inside, too. And then you stick the whole mess in your mouth and chew on it like a cow chewing on a cud. After a few seconds, you'll get a good buzz-rush and want to do a tropical tango. If you use too much lime and cigarette, your heart begins to race, you'll break out in a sweat, and you'll get super nauseous. The grand finale is if you have drunk a bunch of beer along with a hot mix of betel nut, you'll perform the dynamic dual of projectile puking and explosive diarrhea. This is exacerbated even more if you're a naïve white statesider trying to impress your island date. I actually saw it happen once. It wasn't a pretty sight.

For some short background info for my Tinian High School betel nut adventures, I was previously the first white PSS white vice principal at Marianas High School (MHS) on Saipan, which was just before I was picked to lead the island high school from hell on Tinian.

My former principal at MHS was a bombastic shit-for-brains local guy, who got the well-paying job via his well-connected island relatives. The students at MHS really disliked the self-serving SOB and showed it by spitting betel nut juice all over the school buildings, and especially on the principal's office door.

The students knew the principal hated the spitting of betel nut all over "his" campus and he had me instruct the maintenance to make signs that stated the prohibiting of chewing and the dire consequences for those who got caught spitting on the buildings, windows, doors, the principal's car, etc.

It didn't take too long for the signs to be also covered with betel nut juice, and all these spitting shenanigans would be a bigger problem for the principal when the U.S. accreditation team was scheduled to soon arrive and inspect the school.

In desperation, the principal bribed the public works department to quickly whitewash paint the whole school just before the arrival of the U.S. accreditation team, and he even suspended school for a few days prior to the team's visit to prevent spitting on his newly painted school.

The team finally arrived a few days late and I was appointed to give the team a tour of the facilities. Due to the accreditation team's late arrival, the bright red betel nut stains on the walls, windows, and doors were becoming quite visible through the quickie white-wash paint job. Apparently, the public works crew diluted their short supply of paint with plenty of water and the buildings took on the look of a gigantic red poke-a-dotted tablecloth. The school looked like a massive Italian restaurant, and it became difficult for the team and me to not laugh out loud during our tour. I tried my best to explain to the stateside accreditation team about the traditional use of betel nut and how it got out of hand at our school. The team conditionally accepted the cultural action of spitting red betel nut juice on the ground and in the bushes, but why all over the entire school buildings? I replied it was best to discuss this issue with the principal.

This poke-a-dot building issue was, in fact, a strange topic of discussion for the principal and the accreditation team, especially when the matter of discipline and lack of control of students vandalizing school property was discussed.

The principal was very disturbed by this situation and promised to repaint the whole school black and triple the betel nut security on campus. The team didn't quite agree with the choice of black paint, which would look somewhat absurd for an educational institution and it would probably intensify the tropical heat in the school since black adsorbs sunlight. The principal anxiously nodded his agreement and said he had a Plan B or even C. Whatever it took he would prevail in this betel nut war. The team seemed concerned with the principal's maniacal facial expressions as he talked and decided to move on with the odd meeting. I just sat in my chair and kept quiet, fighting hard and biting my lip to not bust out laughing.

Somehow, MHS didn't lose its accreditation, but it was placed on "double secret" probation. I asked one of the male accreditation team members, "How in the hell did our school retain its accreditation with not only the betel nut problems but also the high absenteeism and a revealed hatred for the principal and his dysfunctional administration of the school?"

The team member, who was getting drunk with me at a Hamilton's Bar after a chaotic accreditation visit, just shrugged off my inquiry and said as long as the school's check for the high cost of the accreditation visit cleared the bank, the school would be okay with the unusual probationary designation until the next visit. It also helped the school to get off of double secret probation when a very disturbed principal was later asked to resign.

The next year, when it was my turn at Tinian High School for our first accreditation visit, which I had specially arranged through administrative skill and skullduggery and the fact that we had a thriving 12th grade. I had even conquered the betel nut war by not fighting the students and their island tradition, but I joined them in a peaceful solution.

Way before the accreditation team would visit our school, I had a discussion meeting with my students about the ancient and cultural history of chewing betel nuts. I explained that long before the school buildings and other modern structures were built, the islanders spit on the ground and in the bushes and the rain would wash away the unsightly stains.

So, I made a deal that I would allow betel nut chewing on campus during all the breaks and at lunchtime if the students would respectfully emulate their ancestors and spit on the ground and grassy areas surrounding the buildings.

The clincher was that most of the students didn't realize that I was one of the few outsiders that chewed betel nuts, too. It stunned the students, that at the end of our meeting, I, their fearless principal, tossed a pre-prepared betel nut in my mouth and began chewing, went outside, and spit on the grass.

The strategy worked and there were no more betel nut stains on any of the school buildings or even my truck. Prior to its visit, the accreditation team heard about this unique policy at Tinian High School and it was partly the reason they wanted to make a special visit since every school in our islands had betel nut problems even though it was prohibited to chew on campus.

It was becoming a legend that Tinian High School "allowed" betel nut chewing on campus but amazingly had *no* problems.

Of course, my crazed and goofy commissioner criticized my rebellious behavior of allowing a prohibited school activity, but all the students and their parents supported my unique policy. I won the betel nut battle and when the accreditation team did visit, they were impressed by the clean campus, good student and staff management relationships, no absenteeism problems, and the contented and respectful island students.

Tinian High School was granted accreditation in my first year as principal and our new 12th grade was even given special accreditation status for their graduation from Tinian High School at the end of the school year. This success at THS was met with utter dismay and chagrin from the commissioner, who had earlier sworn that I didn't have a chance in hell to survive one year at the tumultuous and infamously rowdy Tinian High School.

Big Federal Bucks and a Plane, too

Near the end of my first year at Tinian High School, we got a large financial windfall from a federal educational grant. I had to double-check our central office finance office that it was true and, that under the grant's provisions, I was the sole signatory for the 180 thousand bucks. Of course, the Commissioner of Education protested my managing the big bucks, but my buddy the Tinian mayor told the Commish to back off and told him to let the THS principal handle the grant money. The Commissioner feared the Tinian mayor and realized, like most of the people on Tinian, that the mayor was heavy into meth and that he was a big man, who was basically a good guy, but did have a violent temper if you crossed him.

After advising my staff and students of the federal money, I asked them for a wish list. We went nuts since we were a small school and I had the power of the purse strings.

Initially, I bought an entire science lab (lab tables, instruments, class experiments, supplies, etc.) and extra school furniture for the classrooms and the main office. I also bought computers for all ten classrooms, interactive computer systems, and air conditioners for each room. We had a nice ocean bay and protected harbor by the school, so I bought two small sailboats for the student P.E. program. I also purchased bow and arrow equipment and targets. I bought model rocket kits and we had contests for the best and highest-performance rockets. I bought a used 18-foot recreational motorboat and set it up for marine studies and water recreation for the staff and students. The boat was also used to train students for 6-pax boating licenses as future tour operators, and the school was paid boating fees when I transferred the harbor pilots to large ships that needed piloting to our harbor docking facilities. I also bought a used golf cart that I gave to a very pleased mayor for his daily wanderings around the island, since he wasn't allowed to drive.

Finally, my greatest purchase for our high school on a small island was a fairly-priced used Cessna 172 airplane that was in great shape for establishing a student flight program for the students. Even eager parents wanted to get some thrills on a limited entertainment island when I offered free P.T.A. plane rides. I had my pilot's license and I also hired a part-time flight instructor for the students. Even a World War II B-29 Organization adopted our school and offered great support for our plane and college scholarships in aviation for several of our students. If you remember your WWII history, Tinian was the island base for the Enola Gay atomic bomb mission and many other B-29s that were crucial in ending the war with Japan in 1945. I was told that the B-29 organization members appreciated the peaceful aviation activities that were being offered at our school, in contrast to the destructive activities during WWII on Tinian. The organization's members were also grateful that my family and I adopted several memorials to the American military personnel who were stationed on Tinian during the war. My family repaired and maintained the aging memorials that had become adversely subjected to deterioration, bad weather, and the occasional shotgun blast from island vandals.

Needless to say, the jealous commissioner went ballistic, especially after I got great press coverage for having an actual fun and very scholastically functional school in paradise. I was even recommended to be the next commissioner, but I declined saying I was enjoying my adventures on Tinian and didn't want to upset the deranged current commissioner. But alas, the commissioner was truly upset about the talk of my being the next commissioner and he began making his plans for my future administrative demise.

SEALS Rule

The arrival of the U.S. Navy Seal Team in my second year as principal was a classic adventure of a joint military-civilian "statesider" assault on some local thugs on Tinian Island.

One night, as a group of the male white teachers and I were enjoying beers and shooters of tequila at the Kammer Beach Club's outdoor bar, several U.S. military studs in wet swim trunks holding small duffle bags strapped to their waists walked toward us at the bar and asked if they could join us. I asked where in the hell they came from, and they said they had completed their SEAL training maneuvers of swimming ashore from a Navy ship that was anchored about two miles offshore. They were allowed some R&R by their captain once they arrived onshore, and they proceeded to take out shorts, shirts, and cash (no shoes) from the duffle bags that they had brought with them.

About an hour later, the Kammer Beach Club was fully invaded by a stupendously drunk military/civilian squad of adventure-seeking souls. We first started a tackle football game in the bar's sandy sitting area, and we were loudly cheered by a friendly group of imported Filipina "hostesses" from the main building's upstairs brothel.

Later, the SEAL guys wanted to venture out into the island's nightclub district which had a few but rambunctious local bars. Consequently, we teachers agreed to escort them around and, for some weird reason and only known by the tequila gods of crazy, we unscrewed the large lamp globes from the outdoor lighting posts and stuck them on our heads like we were some kind of alien invaders from outer space.

We then walked up the road to the bar that I told the SEALs had the best selection of local young ladies and Filipina waitresses. The young island girls were very pretty and sexy before some got married and put on about 100 pounds from having too many kids and having extra rice and pork feedings.

We arrived at the bar and checked our globes at the door, and we told the local owner we needed to return them later to the Kammer Beach Club. He shrugged like it was just another typical drunken event on Tinian and welcomed our group, especially the well-paid SEALs, who would spend a whole bunch of Uncle Sam's money in his club.

The night was going along real fine, and I even made a great shirt-jacket exchange with one of the SEALs, who was half Comanche and a super cool guy and built like a brick shithouse. He wanted my exotic-looking Hawaiian shirt since he didn't have one, and he traded my shirt for his lightweight leather jacket that he wore as his shirt. I proudly put on the SEAL's former jacket since I no longer had a shirt, and we all continued to happily drink and dance with the local ladies and Filipinas.

However, some local island thugs were very jealous that the local girls and Filipinas were giving all their attention to the SEALs, especially the handsome half-Comanche stud who was simultaneously dancing with three sexy island ladies. Suddenly, three local thugs jumped on the Comanche SEAL and I called out to his SEAL buddies to help their outnumbered SEAL comrade. The Comanche's buddies said don't worry, there are only three guys fighting him. I learned a good lesson that night—never jump on a large Comanche SEAL who has drunk a bunch of tequila fire water, even if you had three or four helpers. Because that night, the Comanche SEAL knocked out all three thugs within just a few minutes.

Several more local thugs started to join the Comanche fracas but soon had a change of heart when two of the thugs went flying across the room with the help of the other SEALs. The SEALs left a whole bunch of money to cover any damages to the club and damages to several local jaws, and thus, ended a great military-educator entertainment exchange night on Tinian.

Yes, we did return the globes and we educators waved to the SEALs from the beach as they swam back to their ship. What a night, and I did return the Comanche SEAL's jacket to him. It had an official SEAL insignia on it, and it wouldn't be right for me to wear it. I went home shirtless because I let the SEAL keep my Hawaiian shirt and had yet another story to explain to my very understanding and patient wife.

School Hillside Fiasco

During my second year, I was directly involved in the selection and approval of the building of a new high school on Tinian because the existing high school was adjoined to the elementary school, and this caused various problems between the older students and younger elementary students.

Being the principal of the high school, I had the final approval of the project, but the approval had to be also concurred by the mayor. Since the giddy mayor enjoyed his golf cart so much, in his meth-induced merriment, he gladly gave me the final control of the school site, the building plans, and the budget.

Per the Request for Proposal (RFP), the school site, building plans, and the budget had been initially reviewed by the PSS Procurement and Supply office on Saipan, and then they were submitted to the Tinian mayor's office following political protocol. Next, the mayor showed me the initial building site and plans and I declined the submittals. He had asked me why, and I said that after I paid for the faulty plans and the worst site ever to build the school, which was on the side of a hill that was owned by a greedy island guy, it would eat up 90 percent of our school's budget to just excavate and level the hillside site and fix the bad plans. It would then leave us with only 10 percent to maybe build a nice student toilet facility. I then offered the mayor a popular alternate site that was situated on *flat* and *free* government land, and I would also not fully pay the local inept architect until he fixed all the screw-ups at no extra charge.

The mayor agreed to the site change because he didn't really like the owner of the hillside but said the school would pay for the changes in the faulty building plans since the local architect was a cousin of his. I "wisely" agreed to pay for the changes to the faulty building plans.

The mayor was so coherently right for once because his cousin the architect was also a vengeful maniac who would have me buried in the concrete poured for the school's foundation if I didn't pay for the corrections in his faulty plans. Concerning the building site, the rejected owner of the hilly site swore he would get me. He did barge into my office later and we had a short physical tussle before the office staff broke up the one-round fracas. My secretary declared me the winner since my drunk adversary slipped and knocked himself silly on the edge of my desk.

It seemed my educational resume was becoming more intriguing as my Tinian High School tenure continued its challenging course of bizarre school activities.

My Last Days on Tinian

Due to the major change of the high school's new building site, it didn't take long for the tropical shit to hit the swaying coconut trees. The islander owner of the costly ex-school site on the side of his hilly property filed a procurement protest against me with the Commissioner of Education. He also accused me of attacking him in my office when he had kindly asked why his expensive hillside was rejected. Furthermore, the local architect, who had to submit corrected plans, filed a harassment complaint against me even though I paid for the changes from the school's budget. The Tinian High School scorecard soon became local islanders: 2; and the white outsider principal: 0.

Later, the commissioner, who wanted to give me payback for previously upstaging him, also falsely accused me of stealing funds from the school's student bank account, which I had earlier closed due to inactivity and the fact it had no money in the account.

What really happened was that I withdrew one thousand dollars of my money from my own bank account to help finish building a student union for the current high school site. The commissioner twisted the story and released it to the media and, subsequently, I was placed on administrative leave and my contract was not renewed two weeks later near the end of my two-year contract.

Since my "at-will" contract was supposedly not fully covered by the local civil service personnel department, I wasn't allowed to challenge the commissioner. The commissioner also stripped me of my higher education scholarship, which was awarded to me for my successful Tinian High School administration work, and which had rewarded me to be accepted in a doctorate program jointly sponsored by the University of Southern California and San Jose State University in California.

What is that famous saying that the road to hell is paved with good intentions? Well, my road to hell was one helluva paved kick in my intentionally good ass.

I had an unemployed wife and two young children, and we were soon sent packing back to Saipan with my being unemployed, too. Plus, my wife was very upset that I had given away our only savings for a school student union building that was completed just as I said goodbye to my nice-paying job on Tinian.

A few days before I left, I drank a bottle of tequila and woke up in the early morning in the school boat that had mysteriously sunk in the harbor in eight feet of water. I woke up floating above the boat since I had somehow put a life preserver on, and once I realized what had happened, I fled the scene.

During packing day on Tinian, my wife gave me a piece of boat equipment that she found in my wet smelly pants that she had washed. It was a hull water plug device that I had apparently pulled out of the school boat's stern section in a drunken stupor, and that's why the boat "mysteriously" sank.

Adios Tinian and Hello Civilization, Again

On our last day on Tinian, my whole family and all our meager Tinian belongings boarded an old military end boat, which was used for hauling cargo between Saipan and Tinian, and I bid an ambivalent adios to Tinian.

After a few days on Saipan, I read in a local Saipan newspaper that it was reported that the Tinian high school boat had mysteriously sunk and it was possibly attributed to a missing hull plug. I still have that plug as a lasting memento of my chaotic days as "Principal of Paradise."

Reflecting on the whole Tinian situation, I did whip the school into a viable and fully accredited high school after adding a 12th grade and improving the overall state of the school. I did so well that it eventually allowed me to be accepted into the joint Doctor of Education cohort program that was offered by the University of Southern California (USC) and San Jose State University (SJSU). Although I was fired again out of petty island vindictiveness at the end of my Tinian two-year contract, which prevented me from receiving a local scholarship to pay for my doctorate program, I again took my severance pay and it barely paid for my travel back to "Civilization" and my first semester at San Jose State University in California in the fall of 1992.

However, due to financial constraints, I had to temporarily leave my first child from a previous Palauan marriage and my current Filipina wife and our little boy with a cleft palate condition on Saipan. I had been further financially rejected for a justifiable U.S. school grant because I was a white guy who presumably shouldn't need financial help in the new era of pissing on privileged white people.

In reality, I was a broke forty-six year-old white guy who needed the doctorate to help my chances to get a decent job in education during an affirmative action era and be able to support my non-white family. White privilege my ass.

Due to a much-needed monetary infusion, I had to settle for an educational loan to allow me to continue my doctorate program and be able to move my family to Victorville in Southern California, which was halfway between SJSU and the USC. To help with our finances, I worked as a part-time security guard and my wife got a job in a Chinese restaurant for us to survive.

Both my island children were enrolled in the Victorville public school system and they had to make adjustments, too. My son, who had a serious cleft palate condition, was placed on a waiting list for the special education school by a fat and arrogant black lady who worked for the Victorville school system. I didn't protest my son's questionable rejection by the black lady and, utilizing my unique island skills to overcome racial adversity, I took my son to the special needs school on the other side of town the following day and walked him to the half-filled classroom. I told the friendly and compassionate special education (SPED) teacher that my son was a new student and his paperwork was still being processed. The teacher observed my shy handicapped little boy and said it was okay and that he can start right away.

A few weeks later, the white SPED teacher said she was still waiting for my son's paperwork, and I just smiled. She had a sense of what happened at the school's administration office, and she smiled, too.

My son enjoyed the opportunity to be with other children, but he did have problems when he was teased about his funny-sounding speech sounds prior to his later corrective surgery for his cleft palate condition.

My daughter had a different problem at her elementary school. The school was in a nice neighborhood, but it had a group of rowdy black kids attending from a rough part of town next to where we lived at the time. Most of the kids in our area took the bus to school, and I walked my daughter to the bus stop in the morning and afternoon. My doctorate classes were scheduled mainly on the weekends due to the fact most of us doctoral students were working people, and

I could care for our children during the weekdays while my wife worked.

One day, I was a little late to the bus stop and saw a strange event take place in the distance. A black boy, who was my daughter's age and size, had jumped on my daughter's back as she was stepping out of the bus. My daughter, who I had enrolled in a community judo class, flipped the boy over and he landed hard on his back. I rushed over, grabbed my daughter, and took her safely home.

The next day, the bus arrived early and I saw my daughter among a group of students waiting for their parents. She started walking toward me in the distance and was suddenly surrounded by a bunch of young black kids who were hiding in the bushes on their way home. The black students would always walk by themselves to their houses down the road from our apartment. I hurriedly ran up to the group and saw the older black kids yelling at a younger boy, who had been tossed off my daughter's back the day before, to kick my daughter's ass. I quickly reached the scene and ordered the older black kids to back away and nodded to my daughter to take care of the problem. She commenced to kick the other black kid's butt with her judo skills and being of half-Palauan descent. Palauan islanders are of Carolinian bloodlines and are rough-and-tumble island people. They have beautiful "Negroid" features and are discriminated against by lighter, brown-skinned islanders in Micronesia. It was ironic to me that my Palauan little girl was being attacked by "Negroid" people in a different part of the world. I was proud of my young daughter's triumph over Black Power.

Unfortunately, two days later, I was summoned to the white principal's office at my daughter's school and I was informed that my daughter was being placed in a racial sensitivity class for a fighting incident that was reported by a black parent. I blew a gasket and told the principal where she could stick her stupid sensitivity class.

Luckily, the black vice principal, who was a young and decent school administrator, had investigated the incident and supported my daughter and me concerning the fight. He also said he would warn the rowdy black kids about not retaliating against my daughter and recommended that the young black students be placed in a racial sensitivity class.

I truly appreciated the black vice principal's support and figured the problem was solved. But a few days later, I was summoned to the Victorville sheriff's office over a fighting incident involving "innocent" black kids that I, the white guy, had instigated.

Again, I was fortunate to later have the school bus driver, who was questioned by the sheriff's office, come to my defense. The bus driver, named Bob, liked my daughter and explained to the sheriffs that she was the victim of a racial attack. I was called back to the sheriff's office and they said the complaint was dropped after hearing the "black" bus driver defending my daughter and me. Doesn't life work in wondrous ways sometimes?

I was a little perturbed later in the week when my daughter came home and asked me to help her with her homework. She had to write a short biography of an important person that the teacher had specially chosen for her. I guess the "racial" fight she had with the black boy, who later became her good friend, curiously affected the teacher's choice. My daughter's selected topic was Dr. Martin Luther King, Jr.

In the midst of barely hanging on financially and being 46 years old, I did receive a sign that I was going to make it when I read one of the Chinese fortune cookies that my wife would hide in her pocket from her job and give to our kids. It said something to the effect that survival can be a bitch sometimes, but you have to hang in there and do what you have to do. Bless you, Confucius, you the man.

The move to California and my being extremely broke was also a blessing in a wondrous disguise because my son qualified for free major medical treatment for his cleft palate condition at the well-known children's clinic at Loma Linda Hospital in Southern California. He had three successful operations to fix his congenital defect, which had caused him severe problems in eating and speaking.

Ironically, after being rejected by the local hospital on Saipan and its mediocre medical facilities, my son was successfully operated on by a nationally known ENT physician. Even in California, island karma can look down kindly upon unfortunate outsiders, and it truly blessed my little boy who is now a successful registered nurse helping other needy patients.

1992-1996

Returning to the U.S. mainland was a cultural and racial shock to me. After living on a small island facing simple and somewhat tolerable social problems, it was a challenge to be tossed into a complex cauldron of social turmoil and racial strife in the Los Angeles area, which was exacerbated by overplayed affirmative action policies and an anti-white sentiment promoted by cowering white politicians and corporate America. It was unnerving to me because L.A. had been my birthplace and in a much earlier time it was a place of youthful fun in the sun.

It's where I grew up body surfing and listening to the Doors while smoking pot and wading through the initial challenges of affirmative action and race quotas. Now I was commuting to the University of Southern California in downtown Los Angeles and facing the prospects of dealing with the dangerous aftermath of the Rodney King race riots in 1992 and later the 1994-95 O.J. Simpson murders and controversial trial.

USC is a beautiful campus, but it was right smack in the middle of a then racially pissed-off black area of L.A, which nearby had continuous racially dangerous incidents during my educational pursuits. My avoiding racial confrontations in and about the USC campus was a very troubling added school "elective" while visiting the hazardous area.

From late 1994 to early 1996, I was pursuing my doctorate in education and I was living in a Big Bear log cabin in the San

Bernardino Mountains. I had to travel three times a week to USC for classes and library research. During this time of school stress and limited funds, my wife and little boy went to the Philippines after his surgeries to live with my wife's family. My little girl went to Hawaii to live with her Palauan mother.

After my late afternoon classes and library time at USC, I spent hours working on my research papers in the all-night computer labs. As a result, I would leave several times after midnight to walk to the off-campus parking lot, which would be sometimes a dangerous adventure. The parking lot was adjacent to some abandoned buildings that were used by several local blacks for drinking and plotting against white folks—because of the dastardly Caucasian actions against Rodney King—and other "We shall overcome" activities.

Unfortunately, on one particular night, a naïve Chinese exchange student stumbled upon the brothers when walking home at night and was robbed. The real bad part was that the Chinese student apparently resisted and he was murdered. Cowardly white USC administrators tried their best to cover up the incident, but other black crimes unfortunately continued against other non-black students.

As for my racial escapades, I remembered one time after midnight I had asked the black security guard stationed on the campus across from the parking lot if he could escort me to my car which was about 100 yards away. I had read that since the killing of the Chinese student and other black muggings around the USC campus, it forced USC to feebly attempt to lessen the black crime. This downplay of black criminal activity tried to placate worried students and to prevent USC from getting a bad reputation for having serious problems with the local black thugs.

USC had slightly increased its security against black crime for mainly ostentatious reasons and to avoid offending the black leaders in the area. As an example of its upgraded security, when I did ask the black security guard to escort me to my car, which was one of the new security procedures for students leaving the campus at night when walking to dimly-lit parking lots, he emphatically replied to me, "Are you crazy, man! It's dangerous out there even for my black ass!"

The security guard did give me some advice on how to "safely" reach my car. He said wait for the brothers to start talking loud and laughing while blasting their hip-hop music. The distractions would allow me to sprint to my car as fast as my white legs would move, and then quickly start the car and get the hell out of the lot. He also said don't stop at any red lights at the intersections, quickly get on the L.A. freeway, and head for home going around 90 miles an hour in order to avoid any blacks on the freeway and also rumors of crazy Mexican gang members, who were harassing and shooting at white drivers on the freeway. The guard further advised me to keep speeding until I reach the white areas outside of downtown L.A.

These late-night, white-legged slow sprints to my car and driving through dangerous L.A. areas were always a pain in the ass. One afternoon at a gas station near the USC campus, I noticed a California Highway Patrol car getting gas. I asked the white CHP cop sitting in his cruiser for advice about my dangerous night-time sprints and expedited travel out of L.A. He looked at me and nonchalantly said get a gun. I thought he was joking, but he wasn't, and he also told me to keep it loaded and easily accessible in case of emergencies.

I then mentioned that having a loaded gun concealed in a car was illegal in California. The cop replied it's your choice. Be legal and dead, or alive and face whatever consequences later. He also reminded me of not only the anti-white problems with the blacks in the area, but he confirmed the rumor that there was a string of shootings of white guys on the freeway in the L.A. area by drugged-up Mexican gang members. I guess the CHP cop was right since some pissed-off Mexicans were seeking revenge for the white gringos stealing California from the Mexicans and for other so-called anti-white reasons.

What the hell was I doing going to USC in the middle of racial Armageddon in downtown L.A.?

Heeding the CHP's advice, I did buy a .357 caliber pistol and it did make me feel somewhat invincible like John Wayne. But frankly, I really didn't want to use it. I just wanted to finish my doctorate program and get back to the islands where the islanders were much less anti-white. The islanders mainly enjoyed fucking with white statesiders when the local government agencies and all their islander employees were requested to assist a stateside outsider when he or she needed to get an island driver's license renewed or tried to get their island shack hooked up with electrical power, etc.

Oh, by the way, I did pull out my .357 pistol once around two in the morning when I was on the outskirts of downtown L.A. on the freeway that was mostly empty of other cars.

Some Mexican low riders decided to screw with me and abruptly pulled in front of me in the fast lane while I was doing about 70 mph. The Mexican driver then slowed down to about 30 mph and I changed lanes, and then he quickly got in front of me again.

What really bothered me was that I had previously read in the newspapers that this type of freeway activity had occurred on other occasions between white male drivers and Mexican gang members. The Mexican driver would bait a white driver, who would possibly react by getting aggressive, and then a Mexican passenger in the other car would open fire with a gun. As a tragic result, a few white guys had been murdered, and now I was an active participant in this dangerous game.

During my dangerous freeway incident, the Mexican driver finally pulled up real close alongside my passenger side. I had lowered my windows down so I could anxiously observe what my Mexican friends were doing. I could clearly see the Mexican driver, who was smiling, and then from out of the back window of the Mexican's car, a small caliber pistol appeared, and I saw Poncho Villa's distant relative smiling at me, too!

I freaked. But I did have my gun ready in my right hand. I leaned over and pointed it out the passenger window and hesitated before I started firing wildly. I had missed hitting the other car because as soon as I pointed my bigger gun out the window, the Mexican driver slammed on his brakes and veered to the opposite side of the freeway.

Simultaneously, I quickly stomped on the gas pedal of my parents' borrowed Ford Thunderbird that I was driving, and soon, I was traveling over 100 miles an hour. I drove for miles at a high rate of speed, hoping I would get pulled over by the CHP.

But eventually, I was out of harm's way and traveling in a white area and slowed down. Score one for John Wayne, but I did have a restless sleep later after I arrived home, and I did change my travel routine at USC. If I was working late in the computer lab, I would locate a lounge area and sleep in a chair until daylight, and then I would safely leave USC and its "exciting" surroundings for my quiet cabin home in the mountains.

These racial interactions did have an effect on my choice of USC research for my dissertation. I chose the rising percentages of criminal activity perpetrated by people of color in America's big urban cities like Los Angeles.

However, my research on this topic during the time of 1993 to 1996 relied on the annual reports on U.S. crime that were compiled by the U.S. Department of Justice (DOJ). My initial findings were very disconcerting. The DOJ was reporting that major crimes, e.g., murder, rape, felony assaults, etc., was committed approximately equally between whites and blacks (roughly 50-50). I then called the District Attorney (DA) offices in the major urban cities, like New York, Miami, Los Angeles, and Chicago, and asked about their city crime reports that were being sent to the DOJ for an overall U.S. crime compilation report published annually by the DOJ.

After talking to the DA data officials about these obvious discrepancies in crime reporting, I discovered why the number of major crimes was split evenly between blacks and whites, which seemed at odds with all the reported criminal activities of blacks in the newspapers and TV news programs.

The reason the white population had a high number of major crimes equal to the black population was that Hispanics (Spaniards, Mexicans, South Americans, etc.) were also included in the white population category. I assumed the DOJ wanted to hide the large disparity between black and white major crimes and surreptitiously placed all "Hispanics" in the white population category, i.e., the DOJ erroneously decided that since Hispanics from Spain were considered "white" by European standards then the DOJ could conveniently turn all brown people into whites.

After uncovering this DOJ spin on the crime data, I again called the big city District Attorneys' offices and further talked to their crime data compilers. It seemed at the time they were instructed by the DOJ to compile their data as the DOJ wanted to politically present to the public, in order to not make the blacks look very bad in the area of criminality.

I recalled one funny comment from a white lady crime compiler in Miami, Florida, who said with a smirk, "Did you know, there wasn't one major crime committed by a Cuban or Puerto Rican all this year in Miami." This was absurdly true because all the Cuban, Puerto Rican, and any other Hispanic crimes were lumped together with the white folks.

Due to public pressure from organizations wanting the true crime statistics by correctly defined racial categories, the categories for criminals were later clearly established as "Whites," "Blacks," "Hispanic non-whites," "Asian-Pacific Islanders," etc.

That's the reason you now read in the comments section of the news articles on the internet that when a male person commits a major crime and they don't mention his race but only give his name as "Jaquan Davontay Johnson," the commenters explode with derisive comments with "we have solved the puzzle." The puzzle being the mainstream media protects the black thugs or the 13 percenters who commit nearly 80 percent of the major crime. The 13 percent is even less if you narrow the category down to black males between the ages of 15 to 30 years old.

Sadly, in the last few years, it's reported that the DOJ doesn't even officially request the annual crime data from the major crime-ridden cities, which further politicizes the corrupt DOJ.

In order to further my research on this Black Power hold on the white cowardly establishment, I decided to visit the L.A. office of the National Association for the Advancement of Colored People (NAACP). To my surprise, I was met by a very cordial and informative NAACP representative who filled me in on a variety of social ills affecting both whites and blacks. I even naively asked if whites could join the NAACP and she laughed and said of course, and she then explained that ironically, a couple of rich liberal-minded white people and a conscientious black lady founded the NAACP.

We proceeded to talk about affirmative action and race quotas, which she said were enforced in Los Angeles—although at times were very unfair to white people. We even discussed sports teams like the Los Angeles Lakers in the National Basketball Association (NBA), which had all black players that year except one token white guy. She said that the Lakers actually violated the L.A. demographic policies of affirmative action and they had created unfair hiring practices that denied whites and even Mexicans a chance of playing for the "all black" Lakers.

I thoroughly enjoyed her frank conversation and opinions so much that I joined the NAACP, and I still have my official NAACP card that placed me in the Beverly Hills Chapter.

And speaking of the Beverly Hills Chapter, I did attend its annual meeting in early 1995 and experienced a very informative get-together of some very disgruntled black elitists at a ritzy hotel in the Beverly Hills area.

Upon arrival at the swanky hotel, I was met at the door by several large and obviously armed black brothers, who curiously looked at my official NAACP membership card and shook their heads at this dumb-ass white boy venturing into their annual anti-white "war council" conference.

I was reluctantly allowed to go in and went directly to the main meeting area to listen to the guest speaker. I sat amongst hundreds of black attendees and did notice I was the only white person in the group, and I was receiving several glances and some menacing stares. I was glad I had hidden my .357 pistol in my heavy coat pocket, although it would have probably been useless as several very militant blacks would have quickly shot the hell out of me if an ugly incident broke out.

Possible future gunplay aside, the main speaker was disturbingly interesting as he delved into the many evil ways that white people oppressed black people. It then got real uncomfortable for me when the speaker's voice began to rise in volume as he stated it would take armed action against the whites to really get their message across. I started to get up to leave, but a kind old black woman grabbed my arm and said, "Stay, you'll be okay." I nervously smiled at her and said I had a class at USC and didn't want to miss an important lecture on the glories of racial diversity.

As I was leaving the meeting, the whole hotel seemed to be blasting the speaker's message for violent rebellion against white oppression. The volume was turned up even higher, and the "kill whitey" rhetoric got much louder and, when I was hurriedly leaving the hotel lobby, a black man yelled at me that it was better that I got the hell out immediately!

So, not to disappoint any of my fellow card-carrying NAACP brothers and sisters, I did get the hell out of there before something really dangerous happened to my physical existence. I guess I wore out my membership in good standing in the Beverly Hills NAACP in about twenty-two minutes.

In my final year at USC, I did change my dissertation topic, but I also decided to jerk the racial establishment a bit. For example, I created a special club at USC called the USC National Association for the Advancement of Caucasian People (NAA"C"P).

I remember setting up my booth in the fall semester of 1995 in the main student area near the statue of "Tommy Trojan." I had some of the most interesting conversations and disconcerting stares from other USC students. Black women were the most interesting and well-mannered in our conversations about racial issues. A few whites were upset that I was causing a disruptive atmosphere and, of course, I had a few black guys who just sat at my booth and glared at me with looks of disbelief and silently saying, "What da fuck is dis shit?"

Another racial adventure I had, with a conditional blessing of my friendly black mentor at the L.A. NAACP office, was that I did sue the L.A. Lakers in the L.A. Federal District Court for racial reverse discrimination and violating L.A.'s affirmative action hiring policies, i.e., in not having the correct proportion of white players on its team as compared to blacks in the overall demographics in L.A. at the time.

I argued in my moving papers that the racial make-up for the Lakers should be 11 whites, 3 blacks, and one Mexican/Asian basketball player. I also argued that since other workplaces and colleges had their institutional standards lowered, which mainly accommodated black people all the time, I wanted the Lakers' basketball standards (the actual basketball rim and backboard) to be also lowered in order to ease the hiring qualifications and creating an "all colors" inclusion standard for the less talented white and Mexican basketball players who couldn't jump as high as their fellow black players. I even cited in my legal argument the movie, "White Men Can't Jump," as a widely publicized example of the Caucasian's plight of being too slow and having less jumping ability than their black colleagues in the game of basketball.

My most crucial argument for the lowered basketball standards at both ends of the basketball court was that the standards would automatically be lowered to make it more accessible when a white player or Mexican-Asian player was attempting a dunk shot. I even provided the court with mechanical drawings of a basketball standard being automatically lowered when it electronically sensed a white guy attempting a low-flying dunk shot.

Needless to say, the L.A. District Court dismissed my case without even the courtesy of a hearing after both sides filed their very emotional and moving papers. I even received a special delivery letter threatening to have me investigated for "stalking" Jerry West, who was a former star of the Lakers and the Vice President of the Lakers at the time. I wasn't stalking Jerry West. He was just the guy who did the hiring, so I sued him for not giving me a chance to be a Laker with the blessing of the "Civil Rights Act of 1964, as amended."

Later, I appealed the dastardly dismissal of my L.A. District Court case to the Ninth Circuit Court of Appeals, which also dastardly dismissed my case in a record time of about three minutes and 52 seconds. [See: *John (Jack) A. Angello, Plaintiff-appellant, v. Jerry West, Vice President of Operations; the Los Angeles Lakers Inc.; California Sports Inc., Defendants-appellees, 76 F.3d 384 (9th Cir. 1996).*]

On a much happier note, I did manage to graduate in June of 1996 with a Doctor of Education degree. I had just enough bucks for some spending money and an airline ticket back to the islands to continue my assault on paradise, whether some of the more bigoted xenophobic islanders liked it or not. I also wanted to get past page three of my screenplay for Mr. Mirisch.

1996-2002

I'm back! I arrived on Saipan in the summer of 1996 with barely 100 bucks in my pocket. My wife, who had been living in the Philippines with our young son, joined me as did my daughter who had been staying in Hawaii with her mother.

We all stayed in a small, one-room shack that had one bed and a tiny toilet. My children were very young and didn't mind the cramped living style.

After a few days, I bought an old Datsun two-door coupe for fifty bucks. It barely ran but it got my wife to work as a cashier for two dollars an hour. I walked all over looking for work and, by a stroke of good luck, the local junior college, Northern Marianas College (NMC), needed at least one teacher with a doctorate degree for upcoming accreditation purposes. And bingo, guess who they had to hire out of need, and not for real "love," since my last island education job ended in my ugly termination by some bigoted islander leaders at the CNMI public school system.

Saipan is a small island and every islander seems related to each other, but I was fortunate that the college president was a very nice islander lady and a former nun who had a very kind heart. She told me that she had been criticized by some of her island colleagues for hiring the stubborn white guy, who kept coming back to find work and live on Saipan.

Instead of the standard two-year contract, I was given only a six-month contract to prove myself worthy and, subsequently, I worked hard and kicked butt as the NMC director of vocational education. I grew up working with my dad in construction in the Los Angeles area, and I was able to create a multitude of NMC programs that benefitted the young, unskilled islanders. I received many commendations from the feds and even local officials, and after six years in 2002, I was about to receive a special federal grant sent to the governor's office from Washington, D.C., in order to expand my successful programs.

However, there was also another special award that I was about to receive. You know the metaphorical story about the crabs that were all scrambling about in a pot of boiling water, and one crab, through determination and grit, made it to the top of the pot to free itself from the fate of falling below into the boiling struggle in order to remain alive and competitive in a rough and tumble life. But then a few jealous and desperate crabs that were also trying to get out pulled the one crab at the top back down and they all fell back into the boiling water.

It's called crab mentality and my good "crabby climbing" work ethic, along with the crabby work of a few other hardworking college crabs, which included statesiders and islanders, caused a group of jealous islander crabs and some kiss-ass white struggling crabs to sabotage us climbers to the top.

We all got eventually terminated for reasons not fully explained, except that it was later revealed that we got mainly booted from the college for indirectly exposing a devious plan of corruption between certain college administrators and certain other local government officials, which involved some big federal bucks. Even our supportive islander president was forced to resign partly due to her support of us hardworking crabs.

AAAAAHHHHHHHHGGGGGGG! It was now back to looking for a job again, which was not that easy for a repeat "terminatee" at age 56 on a tiny island that was full of cranky, struggling crabs.

2003

I spent over a year on Saipan out of work. Meanwhile, the commonwealth civil service did accept my NMC termination complaint and clearly ruled on my behalf.

Later, NMC's local islander attorney appealed the civil service ruling in the Saipan (NMI) Superior Court and, again, I won the case in our Superior Court because my case had clear legal merit on my side.

But I finally lost on appeal to our "local" Supreme Court when the islander government officials and all the islander justices ganged up on me with the attitude, "It's either us islanders or the outsiders."

Some overly xenophobic local islanders love to say, "This is _our_ island, outsiders," even though Saipan is a legal part of a bona fide U.S. commonwealth where all citizens are supposed to be treated equally and fairly.

The case did make the front page of the island newspaper for several days and I won a little sympathy from some local islanders for fighting back against some very biased island politics.

2004-2006

As I earlier stated, I did get some respect for fighting for my job and, fortunately, the island's Attorney General, a tough and very intelligent white woman who had the respect of the islanders for being fair and even-handed, hired me in early 2004 as an office assistant.

I was paid one-fifth of my NMC pay, but it greatly helped me to barely pay the rent and put food on my family's table. I worked hard in the criminal division and soon became a certified paralegal and got a nice pay raise. I even wrote several decent legal opinions that were blessed and signed off by my superiors. This job would later lead me to bigger and better things in the future.

2007-2012

My work in the Attorney General's Office got me noticed by the local legislature and I was offered a well-paying job. My legislative work involved consulting various legislators and I drafted many new bills for committee consideration. Legislative consultants and attorneys were mostly white guys due to their advantage of being more experienced writers of the English language that was used in all legislation.

All in all, I enjoyed the work but felt sorry for the general public who didn't have a clue sometimes of the wheeling and dealing that went on behind the scenes to get special interest legislation passed.

One of my main island goals was to work long enough in the government sector between firings to qualify for the decent government retirement program.

This plan was temporarily interrupted from the year 2008 to 2009 when I moved back to California to care for my ailing parents. Sadly, I lost both of my parents in 2009, and I remember them dearly to this day.

By some miracle, I did qualify in 2010 for retirement and I also worked two years for only 60 days in a year for the legislature without the penalty of double dipping. Thank you, Lord, and the island gods who came to my rescue again!

2013-2023

I was too young to fully retire circa 2012 and doing nothing on Saipan can easily drive you into the island nut house. So, in 2013, I found out about a federal program to teach young students struggling in Math and English. It was a part-time job with a fair salary, and it didn't violate the local double-dipping laws that would have jeopardized my fairly decent monthly retirement payments.

I became a traveling teacher and worked at various schools, and the students were young and mostly rambunctious. But I had taught in my early educational career with a tough love mentality, and I've survived since 2013 to the present doing this gratifying work.

My grown daughter is amazed at my patience to teach youngsters at my advancing age, but I tell her the secret is preparation, staying ahead of the students, and never losing class control or they'll eat you alive.

Teaching is challenging and stressful if you sincerely do a good job helping young minds. Furthermore, after a few stressful years of teaching, I did take an exhilarating break in the summer of 2015, and I traveled to Florida to accomplish a long-time wish of mine. I flew a two-seater P-51 combat fighter plane for nearly an hour in the beautiful and sunny Florida skies with an instructor. Due to the P-51's tremendous power and my lack of experience flying a high-performance plane, I didn't take off and land the magnificent beast.

But I did fly the plane as a pilot in control (PIC) and performed many aerobatic maneuvers that my instructor approved and commended my performance. Yes, old flying dogs can learn new tricks. It was such a joyous kick in the ass that after my flight, it was difficult getting out of the cramped cockpit seat due to my fully stretched and cumbersome erection.

Well, as I close this unabashed and slightly discombobulated autobiography that was finished in the winter of 2023, I'm still battling a white coward's war against a global anti-white movement, which reeks of certain colored people's jealousies and their own self-serving prejudices. Unfortunately, it's also exacerbated by an over-the-top and divisive payback plan motivated by a distorted mindset against so-called white privilege.

On a less serious note, I have to confess that I'm still on page three of my sci-fi screenplay titled "Lunatics, Inc." After forty-plus years, I keep pushing the time frame of my science fiction story ahead a few more years into the future to keep it relevant.

I do plan to finish the screenplay some year soon and overcome a severe bout of tropical procrastination and too much tequila, which I decided to give up after finally leaving a shithole bar on Saipan called "Godfather's" that was managed by a fellow white semi-asshole named Snotty. I want to keep my promise to Mr. Mirisch and will dedicate the screenplay to him for his kind friendship with a struggling ABC messenger driver a long time ago. He turned 101 years old on November 8, 2022, but unfortunately, Mr. Mirisch died on February 24, 2023, and I wish him God's blessings for his lifetime of gracious living and his outstanding entertainment achievements. Finally, if my screenplay ever reaches the Mirisch Agency run by his son, Lawrence Mirisch, I will kindly request his current assistant to glance at the cover page and, if necessary, toss my screenplay into the trash can!

A RANT ON SO-CALLED WHITE PRIVILEGE AND THE SO-CALLED OPPRESSION OF BLACKS IN AMERICA

It's amazing that blacks can bitch about oppression and white privilege in the United States when all I see are the following black privileges: 1) privileged blacks are in almost every TV commercial and they are mostly in contrived white situations—can't wait for the Coppertone suntan lotion company to be forced to replace the little white girl's red sunburnt white butt with a black child's non-red black butt in its famous ad—and where are the Mexican and Asians in this "diverse" advertising world? 2) privileged black athletes making millions of dollars dribbling a ball around a wooden floor, or running around on fake grass carrying a football and meanwhile protesting against the unfairness of white people who created the popular sports of basketball, football, and baseball; aren't blacks guilty of stealing the cultural sport's creations of white guys? 3) privileged blacks making millions acting in almost every movie as always the hero or brainy scientist; 4) privileged blacks being exulted for anything they ever do that is normal for anyone else while being excused for the most criminal behavior in America as they violently attack innocent non-black people and the mostly good police officers, which is always sanitized in the patronizing mainstream media; 5) privileged blacks are monopolizing radio, television, the internet, and social media with all their black privilege demands like millions of dollars in reparations and a guaranteed annual free big bucks salary...and for what? For getting a free ride and massive monetary bucks on the backs of guilt-ridden and cowering whites. Today's privileged blacks in America never had it so good. Ask Puff Diddy. King Lebron James, Oprah, etc., etc. And it's all being promoted by cowering white political leaders, business owners, and executives, who nervously support the notion of "superior" blacks, who can easily appropriate all the cultural achievements and discoveries of white people and other non-blacks without any repercussions or criticism.

As for my own cowering to this Black Power destructive force on all American society, I continue to promise that I will not cornrow my hair or try to rap, as long as the blacks stop misappropriating all the white people's cultural shit and stop being involved in degrading and stupid black ads on TV.

How about this? Why don't black people start inventing or discovering some new things to add to the progress of our society? Rapping, hip-hopping, and trash-talking other people are not new or constructive societal discoveries. These activities were actually appropriated from the African black tribes who did those activities long ago to pass their idle time in primitive villages.

Granted, the beginnings of black living in America were rooted in oppression and bondage, which was created by many culprits and not just white people. Yeah, read authentic history books, which reveal that the majority of the slave trading bastards were actually powerful black tribal chiefs and warriors who traded their weaker black neighbors for money and power. Yeah, check the history of the Kingdom of Dahomey and their active and cruel business dealings in the Atlantic slave trade in the late 1860s.

Subsequently, the modern-day blacks, also known as the rich, gold chain-wearing homies, now live in an opportunistic world of guilt-ridden whites and they love appropriating and hijacking lucrative white people's culture and possessions, while claiming unlimited welfare benefits, operating profitable drug dealing, and pimping without any tangible social or criminal repercussions.

Blacks are also coddled with preferential business opportunities and hiring policies, along with outrageous salaries for exploiting white people's sports and entertainment while misappropriating white people's discoveries like TV, movie making, etc., but still bitch and moan about no opportunities or not enough food stamps.

Even the fantastic hit movie that blacks like to brag about their ongoing creative greatness called "The Black Panther" was actually created by a white guy at Marvel Comics. And, of course, instead of creating their own black stories, they love using black actors in several traditional successful white roles, e.g., "I Am Legend," "Wild Wild West," "The Magnificent Seven," "Cinderella," "Annie," and the list goes on. Where are the black writers coming up with popular and classic stories that make the big bucks?

My favorite black appropriation movie is called "Unstoppable," where Denzel Washington played a real-life train engineer who prevented a major train wreck. The only problem was I researched who the engineer really was, and you guessed it, he was a white guy.

Now let's talk about denigrating "dead white people" and the popular racist activity of revisionist history to shame all white people.

I recently read an interesting news article titled "The War on the West," written by Douglas Murray. He writes about how the respect and celebration of the many achievements of the Western civilization have now been subjected to cultural warfare and, furthermore, the Western civilization has been turned into a historical embarrassment and an anachronistic and shameful period. The multi-colored woke and revisionist assholes flailing against the West are waging a remorseless and racist assault on everything having to do with the Western world—past, present, and future.

The blacks continually complained about being "oppressed" people of color, constantly making one-sided self-serving arguments and spewing false claims of being always unfairly treated. They talk of equality but do not care about other peoples' equal rights. They talk of anti-racism but are deeply racist in their own actions. They speak of justice but seem to mean revenge. They claim there's a theory of "White Replacement," where there is a conspiracy that whites want to eliminate people of color when in real life, there is an actual socio-economic movement of "Black Replacement," where blacks do preach the actual elimination of white people.

Not only do blacks want all the lucrative jobs in sports, entertainment, etc., but they also want to be appointed as all the head coaches, producers, executives, and owners without having to rightfully earn these positions. Oh, I forgot, blacks do want white people to keep filling the stadiums and arenas to pay excessive charges to watch these prima donna blacks dunk basketballs and run around carrying a football and other world-shaking achievements that are "so critical" for our survival. The greatest hypocrisy of black sports privilege was when I recently saw two National Football League teams, who were nearly all black players, playing on the field and wearing their fashionable uniforms that had a pompous "race message" on the back of their helmets, ironically saying "END RACISM." Why not let a more whites and other races play for the big bucks, too? Oh yeah, they're not "athletic" enough.

On the other hand, the Western white world has produced many "miracles" in medicine and other marvelous discoveries and inventions. The Western white world is also responsible for a thriving culture influenced by great philosophers, artists, musicians, sportsmen, and political leaders. Currently, this white era of phenomenal achievements is being characterized as a dysfunctional product of "dead and living white people," and it is met with ridicule, hostility, and even violence. There is even a troubling trend to attack productive Asian people in America by blacks, who resent their hardworking, successful traits and superior intellect in most high-tech and scientific areas.

Unfortunately, even people of color who have integrated well and contributed to the "Western world" are treated as race traitors. Sadly, this cultural warfare in the West is being hatefully promoted by socialistic educators and provocateurs like George Soros who promote Black Lives Matter (BLM), Critical Race Theory, and White Replacement Theory.

Furthermore, the real problem is the mainstream socialistic and ultra-liberal media, and the political pandering by certain despicable Democrats toward vulnerable people of color and the illegal immigrants who are "legally" groomed for more Democratic votes. This corrupt and amoral political behavior is exacerbating a volatile situation that could someday create a dangerous civil war between different races and cultures in America.

Oh yeah, I also think the BLM movement, which was created by opportunistic black leaders and the race-mongering media over the controversial and unfortunate incident of "Saint George Floyd the Innocent Felon," was actually created to fleece big bucks from guilty white people and woke organizations.

The BLM movement should be really changed to the BMM movement, i.e., the "Black Mansions Matter." It has already been exposed about the selfish and sinister activities of the BLM leaders squandering the millions of dollars, which they strong-armed from naïve donors (mostly cowardly white corporations), to buy themselves multi-million mansions, instead of their fake

155

mission to help the "underprivileged" blacks who suffer from the evils of so-called white privilege.

I once read "Why Black People Tend to Shout," written by a late black writer named Ralph Wiley many years ago.

It was an interesting book about all da black people's problems due to all da damn white people. It got me thinking about another interesting title for a more revisionist modern book called: "It's Time That White People Start Shouting and Start Pushing Back All the Damn Crap That They Have Had to Take from Black People Who Love to Shout Shit in White People's Faces and Who Love to Push Cowering White People All Over Da Damn Place!"

"Eeny, meeny, miney, moe, try and catch an illegal alien by his toe at the border as you know..."

Well, that's another modern-day story concerning the mostly disastrous avalanche of illegal "browns" and other ethnicities and the plague of violent criminals crossing America's southern border and threatening the present and future peace and prosperity of the United States and all lives that matter.

Frankly speaking, I firmly believe the only solution to America's growing problem of a complete and irreparable division between conservative people of all colors and liberal people of all colors is a fully separated America into two distinct countries. If this is not accomplished soon, there will be a nasty civil war, which will forever destroy America that we now know is a country composed of two very different and angry political ideologies. It's basically a choice for Americans to choose two distinct Americas, or one extinct America.

To be continued...maybe.

A NECESSARY POSTSCRIPT

I've included a noteworthy and pertinent quote from a great black man I've admired over the years. He was born into slavery in 1856 and endured many years of poverty. But he overcame his handicaps in life and became a famous educator, author, orator, a dominate leader in the African-American community, an advisor to many U.S. Presidents, and founder of the Tuskegee Normal and Industrial Institute—now called Tuskegee University, The quote reads as follows:

> "There is another class of coloured people who make a business of keeping the troubles, the wrongs, and the hardships of the Negro race before the public. Having learned that they are able to make a living out of their troubles, they have grown into a settled habit of advertising their wrongs—partly because they want sympathy and partly because it pays. Some of these people do not want the Negro to lose his grievances, because they do not want to lose their jobs."

> —Booker T. Washington

Booker T. Washington was criticized for his astute beliefs by other hypocritical blacks during his lifetime and in his later years. In particular, he was opposed by W.E.B. Du Bois, a black man who was born in 1868 in a privileged setting and became both an elitist racial manipulator and opportunistic black civil rights leader. Du Bois was a perfect example of Booker T. Washington's exposing of certain black people who don't want other blacks to lose their problems and grievances because people similar to DuBois, like Reverend Jesse Jackson and Reverend Al Sharpton don't want to lose their lucrative jobs, too.

ABOUT THE AUTHOR

Dr. J. Ellwood Augello grew up in Pacoima and San Fernando, California during the early 1950s and through the 1970s. In 1978, he left the confines of civilization and ventured into unknown islands in the vast Western Pacific Ocean. In the last forty-plus years, he has worked a variety of island jobs and traveled extensively throughout Asia and the Pacific islands. He completed his Doctorate in Education at the University of Southern California in 1996 and has been teaching underprivileged students for many years. He plans to "retire" in 2023.

Augello had chosen the isolation of a small tropical island to live and survive in order to complete his three writing projects that he had started around 1975 in California.

He finished his novel "Minorities, Inc." in 2021 under the pen name of Reverend Jussie S. Jackson II, and he completed "Black Power & white cower, Inc." in the winter of 2023. His final project, a screenplay entitled "Lunatics, Inc." should be finished in 2023—possibly. His website is islandasylum.com.

The start dates of his three projects in 1975 and his finishing the writing of all three during the time frame of 2020 to 2023 indicates that he has long been plagued by severe tropical procrastination and too much tequila, which he sadly gave up in early 2020.

Hence, he was finally coherent enough to adequately finish two of his three writing goals in early 2023, with the third project, "Lunatics, Inc., still a work in perpetual progress. Honestly, the author feels his writing isn't that great, and that's okay, because the journey has been well worth it.

www.ingramcontent.com/pod-product-compliance
Lightning Source LLC
Chambersburg PA
CBHW032054040426
42335CB00037B/717